KU-493-318

WATERCOLOR
OIL & ACRYLIC

A PRACTICAL GUIDE TO SUCCESSFUL PAINTING

WATERCOLOR
OIL & ACRYLIC

A PRACTICAL GUIDE TO SUCCESSFUL PAINTING

A COMPLETE STEP-BY-STEP COURSE IN TECHNIQUES, FROM GETTING STARTED TO
ACHIEVING EXCELLENCE, ALL SHOWN IN OVER 420 AT-A-GLANCE PHOTOGRAPHS

HAZEL HARRISON

southwater

This edition is published by Southwater

Southwater is an imprint of Anness Publishing Ltd
Hermes House, 88–89 Blackfriars Road, London SE1 8HA
tel. 020 7401 2077; fax 020 7633 9499; www.southwaterbooks.com; www.annesspublishing.com

If you like the images in this book and would like to investigate using them for publishing,
promotions or advertising, please visit our website www.practicalpublishing.com
for more information.

© Anness Publishing Ltd 1999, 2007

UK agent: The Manning Partnership Ltd, 6 The Old Dairy, Melcombe Road, Bath BA2 3LR;
tel. 01225 478444; fax 01225 478440; sales@manning-partnership.co.uk

UK distributor: Grantham Book Services Ltd, Isaac Newton Way, Alma Park Industrial Estate,
Grantham, Lincs NG31 9SD; tel. 01476 541080; fax 01476 541061; orders@gbs.tbs-ltd.co.uk

North American agent/distributor: National Book Network, 4501 Forbes Boulevard, Suite 200,
Lanham, MD 20706; tel. 301 459 3366; fax 301 429 5746; www.nbnbooks.com

Australian agent/distributor: Pan Macmillan Australia, Level 18, St Martins Tower, 31 Market St,
Sydney, NSW 2000; tel. 1300 135 113; fax 1300 135 103; customer.service@macmillan.com.au

New Zealand agent/distributor: David Bateman Ltd, 30 Tarndale Grove, Off Bush Road, Albany,
Auckland; tel. (09) 415 7664; fax (09) 415 8892

A CIP catalogue record for this book is available from the British Library.

Publisher: Joanna Lorenz
Project Editor: Samantha Gray
Designer: Michael Morey
Photographers: Paul Forrester, John Freeman

Previously published as *Practical Handbook: Painting with Watercolors, Oils & Acrylics*

1 3 5 7 9 10 8 6 4 2

CONTENTS

WATERCOLOUR 7

OIL & ACRYLIC 69

INDEX 126

Watercolour

ABOUT WATERCOLOUR

Since the 19th century, watercolour has been without question the most popular medium among amateur painters, and it continues to hold its position of pre-eminence today. It is not hard to find reasons for this. The rise of the medium coincided with the Victorian love of scenery and the natural world. Landscape and flowers were, and still are, the most frequently painted subjects, and water-colour, with its fluidity, freshness and sparkle, is perfect for both.

It is far from being a medium solely for amateurs. More and more professional artists are turning to watercolour, and their subject matter is less limited. The medium is used for portraits and figure studies, for still lifes and cityscapes – indeed anything which can be painted is painted in watercolour.

WATERCOLOUR IN THE PAST

In fact, there is nothing new about the medium's popularity with professionals. Although we see mainly oil paintings when we visit historic collections of paintings, giving the impression that watercolour was regarded as a poor relation, this was dictated more by market forces than by anything else. On the whole, patrons and

OLIVIA FRASER
VICEROY'S HOUSE, NEW DELHI
(Above) *This striking painting, with its deep, rich colours, quickly dispels one of the common myths about watercolour – that it is a wishy-washy medium. The artist has controlled the paint with great assurance, taking the dark colour of the sky carefully around the edges of the building, and, on the building itself, laying one wash over another to create a patchwork of crisp-edged shapes.*

(Left) *Most watercolour artists own a selection of watercolour tubes and pans.*

JOHN LIDZEY
STILL LIFE WITH CANDLES

(Above) *This artist enjoys the unpredictability of watercolour; he encourages colours to bleed into one another, forming pools and backruns. However, although this still life appears free and spontaneous both in arrangement and in the manner of execution, the artist has chosen and placed the objects to form a pleasing composition, and he controls the watercolour with equal care, using pieces of cotton wool (cotton balls) to halt the flow of colours and to lift out soft highlights such as those on the candle flames and glass.*

RONALD JESTY
KIPPERS

(Right) *Although this painting and John Lidzey's are both still lifes, they could not be more different in approach and technique. Here there are no pools or runs of paint, and each edge is meticulously clean and clear. Jesty likes to try out unusual viewpoints in his still-life paintings, and here he has chosen to look down on the subject so that he can exploit the pattern made by the fish and the dark triangles.*

ELISABETH HARDEN
BLUE INTERIOR
(Above) *Painting interiors is a branch of still-life painting, although the subject is wider – you are dealing not just with objects but with their relationship to the surrounding space, so the perspective must be correct and the composition well-planned. The artist begins with rough sketches to plan the composition, then makes a careful drawing.*

RONALD JESTY
ROCK POOL
(Above) *This artist achieves his crisp effects and dense, glowing colours by working wet on dry, reserving highlights by painting carefully around them. You can see this effect on the background hills, the dark areas of rock and the water, where small patches of light-coloured paint have been left uncovered by later dark washes of colour.*

buyers wanted large, imposing oil paintings, particularly for commissioned portraits, so artists tended to reserve watercolour for their more private works, or for sketches used as reference for oil paintings.

A notable exception to this general rule was a group of 18th-century English painters who worked entirely in watercolour, painting landscapes and seascapes. Most particularly, the work of John Sell Cotman and Thomas Girtin (a genius who died tragically young) is well worth looking at in books of reproductions, as are the watercolours of J.M.W. Turner, whose unconventional and innovative techniques

KEN PAINE
AMELIA

(Below) *At first sight, this expressive portrait might well be mistaken for an oil painting, but in fact it is watercolour with the addition of Chinese white. The artist made no initial pencil drawing, but started immediately with a brush and thin paint, gradually increasing the amount of white.*

JOAN ELLIOTT BATES
FROM THE MULE PATH, SOUTH SPAIN

(Above) *Opaque paint has also been used for this charming landscape painted on location, but in this case it is gouache rather than watercolour mixed with white. The effect is very similar if the gouache is used fairly thinly, as it has been here, although you can achieve thicker, more solid colour if required.*

JULIETTE PALMER
BIRCH TRUNKS

(Left) *In this evocative and intricately detailed painting there is a strong emphasis on the pattern formed by the intertwining trunks and branches. The textures too have been described with great care, with a succession of small, delicate brushstrokes used for the trunks and distant clumps of twigs. The fine highlights in the foreground, which play an important part in the composition, were reserved by painting darker washes around lighter colours.*

are an endless source of inspiration. The giant of watercolour painting in America, at a slightly later date, was Winslow Homer, whose magical landscapes are now accorded the recognition they deserve (in his own lifetime, his oil paintings were better-known).

MYTHS AND PREJUDICES

For some reason, watercolour has attracted a more comprehensive – and often inexplicable – list of dos and don'ts than any other medium. People feel that there is a "correct" way of working and that any departure from this constitutes a kind of unfaithfulness to the medium. For example, we are told that we must never use opaque white because it will spoil the lovely translucence of the colours; while good painting aids such as masking fluid are

TREVOR CHAMBERLAIN
STILL-LIFE SESSION AT THE SEED
WAREHOUSE

(Above) *Figure groups are not the easiest of subjects to tackle in watercolour, as it is not possible to make extensive corrections, but this painting shows that in skilled hands there is nothing the medium cannot do. Each brushstroke has been placed with care and, although the artist has worked largely wet into wet, he has controlled the paint so that it has not spread randomly over the surface.*

ELISABETH HARDEN
MAKING MARMALADE

Here the contrast between warm and cool colours has been skilfully exploited to highlight the dominant colour – orange. Although the colour scheme is deliberately limited, the artist has introduced a range of greens, blues and warm yellow-browns into the shadows to create variety and form colour links which unify the composition.

(Left) *Watercolours are usually painted with the board held flat or at a slight angle, but in this on-the-spot painting the artist has worked with the board upright on an easel, causing the paint to run down the paper at the bottom of the picture. She has left the foreground otherwise undefined – the runs of paint hint at reflections in water.*

MIKE BERNARD
COW PARSLEY AND HOUSE
(Below) *Bernard seldom uses one medium on its own; here he has combined watercolour with expressive pen drawing. This has allowed him to introduce touches of detail into the foreground while keeping both the drawing and the watercolour washes unrestrained. The heads of the cow parsley are ink blots dropped from the pen, which have spread in places into the surrounding colours, and the linear highlights were achieved by scratching into dry paint.*

described as "mechanical" and therefore in some way immoral. Eyebrows are raised if you try anything new – it is simply not done. Interestingly, all these theories of correct procedure have only sprung up in this century, while the more rigid rules surrounding oil painting were the product of 18th- and 19th-century academic tradition and have since been largely abandoned. The best 19th-century watercolours, particularly those by Turner, reveal an enormous variety in the methods used, as well as many practices which might be frowned upon today. Turner used opaque paint; he moved the paint around on the picture surface and allowed colours to run; he smudged paint with his fingers and even scratched into it in places. In short, he used the medium as the servant of his ideas rather than the other way around.

The other myth about watercolour is that it is a particularly difficult medium to use. It is true that once you have made a mistake it isn't always possible to put it right, plus, of course, it can be hard to paint in the way that someone else thinks you should. Producing a good painting is never easy, whatever medium you use, but, once you have found your own way of working, the difficulties will be minimized.

PAINTS & BRUSHES

One of the many delights of watercolour is that initially you don't need a great deal in the way of materials: a small paintbox of colours, a few brushes, some paper and a jar for water, and you can make a start. The materials and equipment listed here are the basics; as you become more experienced and develop your own style and way of working, you may want to try out special brushes or a particular kind of palette, therefore it is best to start simply and build up as you go along.

THE PAINTS

Watercolours are produced in tubes, pans and half-pans; the only rather hard decision to make if you are starting from scratch is which to buy. Both have their advantages and disadvantages. Tube colours enable you to make strong, bright colours and to mix up a lot of paint quickly (ideal for those who work on a large scale). However, they are slightly tiresome for outdoor sketching as, unlike pans, they don't fit neatly into a paintbox. Pans are perhaps the most popular choice. They control the paint neatly so that colours don't run into one another, but it is more difficult to release the paint; indeed, you may have to scrub with your brush for some time to produce enough colour for a large wash.

Whichever type you decide on, do make sure that you buy the best-quality paints, known as "artist's" colours. Most manufacturers produce inexpensive ranges, sometimes called "student's" colours and sometimes given a name coined by the particular manufacturer. These usually contain a smaller proportion of pigment than artist's colours and are bulked out with fillers, sometimes making it impossible to achieve any depth of colour or to avoid patchiness, particularly over large areas.

WATERCOLOUR PALETTE

WATERCOLOUR PANS

WATERCOLOUR BOX

WATERCOLOUR TUBES

PAINTBOXES AND PALETTES

The kind of paintbox or palette you choose will depend on whether you are using pans (or half-pans) or tubes. For pans, you need a paintbox specially made for holding them in place, either with divisions for each pan or one long slot in which they all sit side by side. If you opt for tubes you must buy a separate palette or several small ones – or use an improvised palette such as an old plate. At one time you could buy metal paintboxes with small compartments into which the paint was squeezed; these have largely disappeared now, though you might still be lucky enough to find one.

BRUSHES

The best brushes for watercolour work are undoubtedly sables, but they are not recommended as part of a "starter kit" because they are prohibitively expensive, at least in the larger sizes. There are now many synthetic brushes, as well as sable and synthetic mixtures; brushes made from other soft hair such as ox and squirrel are also available. You may find you want to invest in one or two sables later on; if so, take heart from the fact that they are almost literally an investment – they will last a lifetime if you look after them.

Brushes are made in two basic shapes: round and flat. The former are essential, and you will probably require three different sizes: a small one for detail and two larger ones – the size will depend on the scale on which you work. Large flat brushes are useful for laying washes, but you won't need more than one to start with. There are other types of brush, such as mop brushes, which are also good for washes, but like sables these are expensive and should be regarded as a luxury item. You may want to invest in them later on.

COTTON BUDS

SELECTION OF WATERCOLOUR BRUSHES

WATERCOLOUR SPONGES

OTHER ITEMS

Most watercolour painters have a small natural sponge in their box of equipment, which can be used for "lifting out" paint and for mopping up paint that threatens to run. It is also a good alternative to brushes for laying washes. Of course, you also need a jar to hold water, and paper.

FLAT WATERCOLOUR BRUSH

PAPER

Watercolours are nearly always done on white paper; you can work on coloured paper, but this is the exception rather than the rule. The luminous quality that attracts so many people to watercolour work is the result of the white paper reflecting back through the layers of transparent paint. Colours are made lighter by using the paper as the white – heavily diluted paint allows much of the paper to show through, while thicker paint covers it.

PAPER SURFACES AND WEIGHTS
Basically there are three types of watercolour paper: rough, medium rough and smooth. They are all machine-made and are given names derived from the method of production. Rough paper has no alternative name, but smooth paper is known as "hot-pressed" and medium paper as "Not" (i.e. not hot-pressed), or sometimes as "cold-pressed". There are also handmade papers, which vary widely in texture. These are expensive and not always easy to handle; they are best left until you have gained a considerable degree of skill.

The vast majority of watercolour painters, amateur and professional alike, use Not surface paper. This has a slight texture, which holds the paint in place but does not break up the colour. Rough paper can be hard to manage, as the heavy texture tends to interfere with detail, and smooth paper can produce blotchy effects because the paint slides about on it.

All these papers are made in different weights, expressed as pounds (lb). This refers to the weight of a ream of paper – 500 sheets. Weights vary between 70lb, which is very thin, and 300lb, which is so thick that it resembles board. The thicker the paper the more it costs, but very thin paper must be stretched first.

STRETCHING WATERCOLOUR PAPER

Stretching the paper before use prevents it from buckling when you put on the wet paint. Colours laid over ridges and bumps may take a long time to dry out – and sometimes never do so, thus spoiling the effect of your finished work. Paper which is lighter than about 200lb usually needs to be stretched, particularly if you use a lot of wet washes or work wet into wet. The paper used for most types of watercolour sketching pads is 140lb, which will certainly buckle if you work on a large scale and build up many layers of colour, but it is reasonably safe for small-scale outdoor work.

1 ROUGH 2

1 *Soak the paper for a few minutes in a bath or sink. When you are sure it has absorbed the water evenly, lift it out by one corner, shake off the excess moisture and place it on the drawing board.*

2 *Cut four pieces of gumstrip, one for each side, and dampen well by running them across a wet sponge. The gumstrip should be 2.5 cm (1 in) wide for an average-sized painting and up to 5 cm (2 in) wide for a larger one.*

3 *Place a piece of gumstrip along one long edge of the paper and smooth it out firmly from the centre, to ensure that it makes contact with both paper and board at every point.*

4 *Repeat the process for the second long edge and then each alternate short edge. Don't worry if the paper begins to buckle slightly; it will dry flat.*

'E NOT   4 HOT-PRESSED   5, 6, 7 AND 8 TINTED NOT
LB)

GUMSTRIP

Colour

ADVICE ON MIXING

The first and perhaps the most difficult skill to master in any painting medium is mixing colours. Not only do you need to analyse the colours you see, you must also learn to think of them in terms of paint colours. It is easy to say that a sky is blue or that grass is green, but which blue and green would you choose from your paintbox? Which other colours could you mix in to achieve the effect you can see in your subject?

Most of this comes with experience and, it has to be said, after a certain amount of trial and error. But it is useful to know some facts about the paint colours themselves in order to understand what may or may not happen when you mix them.

PRIMARY AND SECONDARY COLOURS

Red, blue and yellow cannot be produced by mixing other colours, so they are called the primary colours. When mixed in pairs, these make the secondary colours: green

from blue and yellow; purple from blue and red; orange from red and yellow. But there is a slight complication here because the primary colours are not absolute – if you look at the starter palette below you will see that there are three different versions of each blue and yellow and two of red.

So before you begin to mix secondaries, you need to know which are the best primary colours to choose to mix the exact shade you want. All colours have different biases, or leanings towards other colours. Of the two reds in the starter palette, for example, one (cadmium red) is vivid and slightly yellow, while the other (alizarin crimson) leans towards blue. To mix bright secondaries you must choose the two primaries that are biased towards each other. Thus ultramarine (red biased) and alizarin crimson make a good purple, but ultramarine and cadmium red do not. For more muted secondaries, choose primaries which have an opposing bias.

Making bright mixtures
The mixtures shown here have all been made from two primary colours which have a bias towards each other. The resulting colours (secondaries) are all vivid, excepting the olive green.

Making subtle mixtures
Here primaries which have an opposite bias combine to make more muted mixtures.

Mixing browns and greys
Different permutations of the primary colours can produce a wide range of tertiary colours – browns, greys and muted greens. The proportion of each colour will depend on the mixture you are aiming at and on the strength of the individual colours – some pigments are stronger than others.

A STARTER PALETTE

The vast range of colours produced by paint manufacturers can be very bewildering for the beginner. How do you choose from this profusion, and how many colours do you need? In fact you don't need very many because you generally have to mix colours to produce equivalents to those you see in the real world. This suggested palette contains twelve colours, which may be over-generous – some of the great watercolourists of the past used no more than three or four.

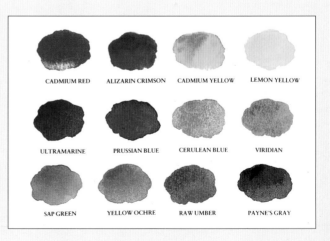

CADMIUM RED   ALIZARIN CRIMSON   CADMIUM YELLOW   LEMON YELLOW

ULTRAMARINE   PRUSSIAN BLUE   CERULEAN BLUE   VIRIDIAN

SAP GREEN   YELLOW OCHRE   RAW UMBER   PAYNE'S GRAY

| CADMIUM RED | MIXTURE | CADMIUM YELLOW | | ULTRAMARINE | MIXTURE | ALIZARIN CRIMSON | | LEMON YELLOW | MIXTURE | PRUSSIAN BLUE |

| CADMIUM YELLOW | MIXTURE | ULTRAMARINE | | CERULEAN BLUE | MIXTURE | LEMON YELLOW |

| LEMON YELLOW | MIXTURE | ALIZARIN CRIMSON | | PRUSSIAN BLUE | MIXTURE | CADMIUM RED | | LEMON YELLOW | MIXTURE | ULTRAMARINE |

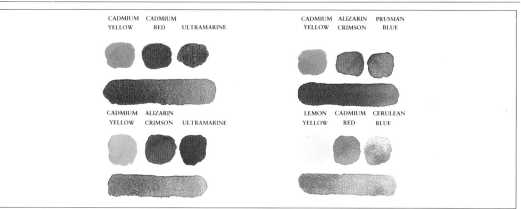

TERTIARY COLOURS

A secondary colour is a mixture of two other colours; when a third colour is added, the result is known as a tertiary colour. These are the so-called neutrals – the browns, beiges and "coloured greys" which play an important part in painting. There is no recipe for mixing these colours because there are so many possible ways of achieving them, but an interesting and varied range can be created simply by mixing three primary colours in different proportions.

WHY MIX?

You may wonder why it is necessary to mix secondary and tertiary colours at all when there are so many ready-made greens, purples and browns. But even if you were to buy a whole manufacturer's range you would seldom have exactly the right colour; furthermore, mixed colours are more subtle and more convincing than bought ones simply because you are making them up yourself, in direct response to a subject.

It is not always necessary to mix completely from scratch. The starter palette contains two secondary colours (the two greens) and two tertiary ones (raw umber and Payne's gray), all of which form good foundations for mixtures and can sometimes even be used as they are in certain areas of a picture. However, you would be well advised to practise colour mixing as much as possible, making charts like the ones shown here, as this will give you the hands-on experience for which there is no substitute.

A Painting in Six Primaries

Making colour charts like those shown on the previous pages will help you to devise useful colour mixtures, giving you valuable experience in handling the medium; but the best way to learn to paint is to do it – that is, to paint an actual subject, choosing and mixing the colours accordingly. The idea behind this exercise is to discover whether you can make all the secondary and tertiary colours that you need for your work by using only the primary colours – two reds, three blues and three yellows.

You can choose any subject that appeals to you, but don't make it too complicated. You could set up a simple still life like the one shown here or, if you like to paint landscape, you could work from a photo-graph. Another alternative would be to copy a painting you like from a book of reproductions. There is nothing wrong with learning by copying. In this case, as you are only using six colours, your copy won't be exact; it will be what is known as a "transcription".

COLOURS USED *cadmium red, alizarin crimson, cadmium yellow, lemon yellow, ultramarine, Prussian blue*

1 Having begun with a light brush drawing in yellow, the artist now paints in the shadow beneath the plate. This warm colour, mixed from cadmium red with small touches of ultramarine and lemon yellow, will later be modified by other colours laid on top.

2 The lemons present no problems, and the colours for these first washes do not require mixing. The lighter areas are pale lemon yellow, and the darker ones a stronger solution of cadmium yellow. Again, shadows will be added at a later stage.

3 Here the amount of water added to the colours is crucial. The paler pink at the top of the apple is well-watered alizarin crimson; beside this is a slightly stronger wash of the same colour, while for the body of the apple the crimson is more concentrated. Now a little blue is added to darken the red and tone it down slightly.

6 (Below) *Final touches were added to darken the shadowed side of the lemon with a well-diluted mixture of ultramarine, lemon yellow and cadmium red, and to build up the forms of the other fruit with darker shadows. It is usually wise to avoid combining more than three colours, as this can make the mixture muddy; the majority of the mixtures here are of only two colours.*

w

W
A
T
E
R
C
O
L
O
U
R

4 *The grey for the plate is mixed from ultramarine with small additions of lemon yellow and alizarin crimson, while the limes are mainly lemon yellow and Prussian blue, with light overlays of ultramarine for the shadows. These have been painted wet into wet so that they merge gently into the greens.*

5 *The same grey as that used for the plate is now washed over the original pinkish colour seen in Step 1. In watercolour work, colours are not only mixed in the paintbox or palette, they can also be modified and altered on the paper by laying one wash over another.*

LAYING WASHES

Basically, watercolour painting is the process of building up a picture through a series of washes of paint diluted with water. A wash can cover the whole of the paper, half of it (perhaps for a sky) or just a small part; it can be roughly defined as colour that covers a wider area than an individual brushstroke could. In the later stages of a painting, definition may be added with small brushmarks or fine lines, but the washes come first and, because they are central to painting in watercolour, the first skill you must master is that of laying a completely even wash of colour.

MIXING COLOUR FOR A WASH
Washes must be laid quickly to prevent hard edges from forming. You cannot stop to make up more colour, so you must ensure that you have enough – washes use up a surprising amount of paint. The paint should be added to the water, not vice versa, but don't start with a large amount of water, or you could waste a good deal of paint achieving a strong enough mix. Instead, put a small amount of water into a saucer, palette or paintbox, pick up some colour with a moistened brush and stir it into the water. If it looks too light, add more paint, and if too dark add more water, repeating the process until you have the depth of colour you require. Stir the paint in well with the brush each time so that the particles of pigment are thoroughly dissolved and there are none left on the brush, otherwise you will have unsightly

DAVID CURTIS
SAILING BOATS
(Below) *The clear, pale sky behind the boats is achieved with a flat wash of watercolour.*

Flat wash on dry paper

1 *The wash has been mixed in a jar rather than a paintbox because it is intended to cover a large area. Watercolour dries much lighter than it appears when wet, so the colour is tested on a spare piece of paper and allowed to dry before the wash is laid.*

streaks of colour. Before laying the wash, check the colour by painting some on a spare piece of paper and letting it dry. Watercolour becomes much lighter as it dries, and the colour may not be what you originally expected.

LAYING THE WASH
The kind of brush you use is a matter of personal preference. Some artists like a large round brush, others prefer a flat one, and some eschew brushes altogether and lay washes with a sponge. Whichever "tool" you use the method is the same. Unless you are using very heavy paper it should first be stretched on a board and propped at a slight angle. The brush (or sponge) is then swept right across the paper from one side to the other; as soon as this first band of colour is in place, the brush is recharged and another band laid below, slightly overlapping the first. This process is repeated until the whole area is covered.

The tilt of the board encourages the paint to run down the paper so that each new "line" of colour mingles with the one above. Some artists like to dampen the paper with clean water before laying a wash, to encourage the colours to blend and to avoid any lines forming between bands. It is worth trying out both methods in order to discover which you prefer.

2 *The board, on which the paper has been stretched with gumstrip, is propped at a slight angle, and the brush is taken smoothly from one side to the other.*

3 *Several successive bands of colour have now been laid. The angle of the board encourages the paint to flow downwards into each new band, so there are no perceptible boundaries.*

Flat wash on damp paper

1 *The paper is first dampened all over with a small natural sponge, which is a vital piece of equipment in watercolour work.*

2 *The way the paint runs down the damp paper can be alarming initially, but it will dry perfectly flat. This is a quick, effective method for covering large areas.*

Laying a flat wash with a sponge

1 *Again working on damp paper, the sponge is taken from one side to the other. At this stage it is hard to believe that it will dry flat.*

2 *But it has. Because the paper was dampened, the darker areas of colour have flowed into the lighter ones, and the earlier irregularities have completely disappeared.*

Laying a gradated wash

1 *A band of full-strength colour is laid across the paper as usual; for each successive band the brush is dipped into the water and then into the paint mixture.*

2 *For artists who are interested in landscape painting this is the most useful type of wash, particularly for skies, which are usually lighter at the bottom.*

Laying a variegated wash

1 *Three colours are to be used and have been mixed up separately. The green touches the blue above so that the two colours blend together with no hard edges.*

2 *On this occasion the board is held flat and the paper is dry. The effect relies on the colours remaining distinct; on damp paper they would flow into one another and mix.*

GRADATED WASHES

Skies are darker at the top than the bottom and a colour wash should reflect this. Laying gradated washes, as they are called, is more difficult than laying flat ones; the need to make the colours progressively weaker or stronger can result in a stripy effect if you are not careful. You can work from light to dark, adding more paint for each band, but it is much easier to control the effect if you begin with the full-strength colour and add more water each time. If you want a wash which is darker at the bottom, simply turn the board upside down and work in the same way.

For each new band of colour, dip the brush into the water before dipping it into the paint in order to weaken the wash mixture by exactly the same amount each time. For a more obvious gradation, you can dip the brush twice into the water, or even use water alone for the second band, in which case the colour from the bottom of the first band will flow into the dampened area, thus creating a paler shadow of itself. Gradated washes must always be done on dry paper, otherwise the different strengths of colour will even out.

VARIEGATED WASHES

Washes frequently contain more than one colour. For instance, an area of grass in a landscape might vary from blue-green to yellow-green, or the sea could contain distinct colour fluctuations. In this case you need to mix in advance all the colours you require, washing your brush between each new colour to keep it pure.

Multi-coloured washes can be controlled quite precisely as long as you test all the colours on spare paper before you start. If you are aiming for a perfect blend of colours, with no obvious boundaries, it is best to work on dampened paper; a frequent feature of such washes, however, is that they are not regular and perfect – it all depends on what you want. You can also make exciting random effects by dropping new colours into a still-damp wash, a technique known as wet into wet, which is discussed later.

COMPLICATED EDGES

Laying a wash to cover a piece of paper entirely is easy enough once you have got the hang of it, but how do you lay a wash that starts and stops exactly where you want it to? You may, for example, want to lay a wash for a sky, below which is a complex skyline of buildings or trees which must stay clean, because it is to be painted in different colours.

In fact, this is much easier than it sounds, but it does rely on making a good drawing to establish exactly where to stop the wash. There are two ways of working and the one you choose depends on whether you like to lay washes on damp or dry paper. If you prefer the former, simply dampen the paper in the area of the wash only, taking a wet brush carefully around your drawn outlines. Lay the wash as usual and it will stop obediently at the dry paper. If you want to lighten the colour slightly and ensure a smooth and even texture, then dab it with blotting paper which will absorb some of the excess paint.

The other method is to work upside down, taking the colour around the edges first. If you want a wash which is darker at the top, leave the board to dry upside down and at an angle; the colour will flow down – that is, up in terms of your picture.

Tricky edges: method 1

1 The wash is to be laid on the sky but not the hills, so the paper has been dampened in the sky area only. The paint stops flowing as soon as it reaches the edge of the dry paper.

2 Notice that the sky wash has dried completely flat. The paper is now dampened again, this time between the sky and the buildings, and a loose multi-coloured wash is laid.

Tricky edges: method 2

1 The board is turned upside down and a deep blue wash laid around the line of the roofs. A round brush with a good point is best for this method.

2 The board has been tilted so that the paint flows downwards, that is, to the top of the sky area. It is left to dry in this position.

MAKING AN UNDERDRAWING

Unless you are just making quick sketches or coloured "doodles" to try out techniques and colour effects, it is important to start your work with a plan of campaign, which means a drawing. This establishes where to place the first washes and which areas to reserve for highlights. Bear in mind too that it is not easy to make major corrections to watercolours, so an initial drawing will save frustration later on.

You may groan at the idea, because it prevents you from getting down to what most people regard as the fun part of the exercise, which is putting on the colour. Also, of course, it seems a waste of valuable painting time – if you are working out of doors, every second counts. You may find in such cases that it is better to make the drawing on one day and paint on the next. Changing light is less important when you are drawing than when you are painting.

Too elaborate a drawing is unnecessary and you should keep it faint, otherwise the pencil marks may show through the lighter areas of colour. Avoid shading and try to restrict yourself to outlines, while making sure that you know what the outlines mean. If you have to amend the drawing, erase the wrong lines as soon as you are confident that the drawing is correct. Take care over erasing as the surfaces of some papers become scuffed rather easily, causing unpleasant blotches when the paint is applied. Use a soft plastic eraser or a kneaded putty one, keeping the pressure light to avoid spoiling the paper surface.

Making a pencil drawing

1 *The artist is using a fairly soft pencil (4B). Anything harder than a 2B could indent the surface of the paper, and is less easy to erase if you make a mistake.*

2 *(Right) The drawing has been kept to outlines only, but the lines are strong enough to provide a guide for the applications of paint. If the drawing is too pale it will quickly become obscured by the first washes.*

Squaring up

1 *A grid of squares has been drawn over the photograph, and a larger grid is now marked out on the paper. Numbering the squares is important, as it is easy to make mistakes when transferring the visual information.*

2 *(Right) Referring to the numbers and letters, the artist redraws the image, taking care to assess where each line intersects with a line on the grid.*

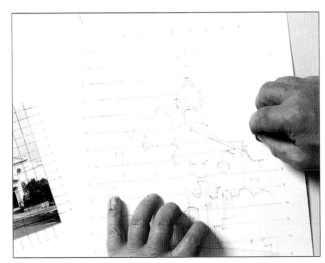

3 *The grid lines are erased in the areas which are to be light in the painting because they would show through pale washes. A putty eraser is used to avoid any risk of scuffing the paper.*

If you are working from a photograph (and don't be ashamed, because many artists do), you can enlarge the image and transfer it to the painting surface by a tried-and-tested method called squaring up. Using a ruler, draw a measured grid over the photograph and then another one, with larger squares, on the paper. You will have to work out the sizes of the squares mathematically according to the size you want your picture to be. For example, if those on the photograph are 1.3 cm (½ in) and those on the paper are 2.5 cm (1 in), the painting will be twice the size of the photograph. Once you have drawn the grids, simply transfer the information from one to the other, checking carefully to see where each line intersects a grid line. This is well worth the effort for any complicated subject, such as architecture, where one wrong angle can throw everything out. It is actually much easier for the eye to judge the exact angles of a subject by comparison with the straight right-angles of a grid.

WORKING WET ON DRY

Watercolour paints are transparent, and consequently paintings are built up in layers, working from light to dark. It is seldom possible to achieve a really dark colour with just one wash, because the paint must be diluted with water in order to spread, and the white of the paper will always show through to some extent. Thus the darkest colours are achieved by laying one wash over another until the required depth is achieved. This layering method, known as wet on dry because each wash must be fully dry before the next is added, is the "classic" watercolour technique. When each wash dries, it forms hard edges at the boundaries; these edges are a positive feature of wet-on-dry painting, adding crisp energy to the image.

The method relies for its success on careful planning. It is not wise to pile on too much colour; as a general rule you should limit yourself to not more than three overlaid washes, as otherwise the colours will begin to lose their clarity, becoming stirred up and muddy. Thus when you begin a painting you need to have a clear idea of what the finished work is to look like, as only in this way can you estimate the depth of colour you need for the first washes. Overlaid washes should always be restricted to relatively small areas of the picture.

You also need to plan the highlights. As you already know, the white in watercolour comes from the paper. White highlights are achieved by "reserving", which means leaving the shape as white paper and painting around it. Highlights are not always white, but areas of a light-coloured wash can be reserved in the same way, by leaving parts showing through overlaid washes. White highlights can be added in opaque paint, but for purity and sparkle you can't beat unblemished white paper.

Overlaid washes

1 *The reflective surface produces blues and whites among the browns, so the artist has begun with a grey-blue wash, slightly darker in the shadow areas, reserving the areas of pure white highlight by painting around them.*

2 *Each wash must be completely dry before the next one is painted on top, so a hairdryer is used to speed up the process. This is a very useful piece of equipment when working indoors.*

3 *The same light brown used for the top of the teapot is now introduced at the bottom. It is best to work from top to bottom whenever possible, to avoid smudging wet paint.*

6 (Above) *Shiny surfaces reflect light and shadow from their surroundings, creating very sharp and distinctly shaped areas of light and dark. The crispness produced by using the wet-on-dry technique is ideal for conveying these qualities in a painting.*

4 *A darker mixture of the same brown is used for the shadowed areas. Notice that, on the lid of the pot, an area of blue-grey formed by the brown painted over the blue in Step 3 has been carefully reserved as a highlight.*

5 *The darkest colours are left until the final stages and placed very carefully. These shadows, like the highlights, define the form of the object.*

WORKING WET INTO WET

This method, which involves applying new colours before the first ones have been allowed to dry, is often regarded as a "special" method, quite separate from the classic wet-on-dry technique. In fact, although some artists do paint whole pictures wet into wet, it is perhaps more usual to see the two methods used in conjunction with one another.

Painting wet into wet is enormously enjoyable. One of the delights of water-colour is its unpredictability, and here the medium is at its tantalizing best – you never know exactly what will happen. Surprisingly, when you drop one wet colour into another, they do not mix completely. The weight of water in the new brushstroke pushes the first layers of paint away slightly, so that the colours mingle and "bleed" into one another, while still remaining separate to an extent. This can create very exciting effects, which vary according to how wet the paint is, the kind of paper you use and

Working on dry paper

1 *Whether you work on pre-dampened or dry paper depends on how thorough you want the wet-into-wet effect to be. Here the artist needs a crisp edge at the top of the hills, and therefore uses dry paper.*

2 *Several applications of paint have by now made the paper thoroughly damp, and the green applied in the foreground spreads out and diffuses. To control the spread of colour, the artist applies the paint lightly, with the tip of the brush.*

Controlling the flow

1 *The paper has been dampened, two colours laid side by side, and the paper lifted and tilted to the left so that the red runs into the blue.*

2 *(Right) A stronger blue has been dropped in at the top and the paper is now tilted so that the colours run down. The paper should normally be stretched for wet-into-wet work, but this is very heavy paper which does not buckle.*

3 *The paper has now been damped only in one area so that the blue paint does not spread below the boundary of the cloud. The tip of the brush is used to create a slightly streaky patch of sky.*

4 *(Above) The same method is used for the large cloud, with dark mauve-greys introduced into a lighter wet wash. Smaller, paler clouds are now touched in above the horizon, again with the tip of the brush.*

5 *(Left) The soft effect of the wet-into-wet painting is enhanced by the occasional crisp edges. Parts of the wall and the small tree have been painted wet on dry, while the cloud has formed a jagged edge where the wet paint met dry paper.*

the colours themselves (different pigments have different "behaviour patterns"). The main problem with the method is that you can't control it very precisely – the paint continues moving until it has dried, and you often find that you cannot preserve a particular effect. You can exert some control, however, by tilting the board so that the paint runs in a certain direction. Artists who paint extensively wet into wet will sometimes move the board around until they have achieved the flow of colours they want; they then use a hairdryer to hasten the drying process and thus "freeze" the picture at a specific moment.

Wet into wet can create a lovely soft atmosphere and, for this reason, is often used for landscapes and weather effects. It can, however, look *too* soft, giving the painting a distinctly woolly and nebulous appearance, so sharper details are usually painted wet on dry as a final stage. You can also add an extra dimension to any subject by working wet into wet in small areas only, thus contrasting soft, blurred edges with the crisper ones made by wet-on-dry washes.

BRUSHWORK

People do not always think of brushwork in connection with watercolour. So much emphasis is placed on the importance of laying flat washes that this aspect of painting tends to be overlooked, but, although brushwork in general is less obvious in watercolour than in a thick, buttery medium like oil, it still has a place. Sometimes it is restricted to the final defining details in a painting. In a mainly wet-into-wet landscape, for example, some light flicks of the brush can suggest foreground grass or the branches of trees, in contrast to softer blends of colour elsewhere in the picture.

Brushwork is more important in the classic wet-on-dry method because of the possibilities presented by the hard edges formed by overlaid washes. These "washes" can take the form of individual brushmarks: perhaps small dabs to suggest the foliage of a tree; calligraphic squiggles to describe reflections in water, or sweeps with a broad brush to follow the direction of clouds in a windswept sky. Some artists lay almost no conventional flat washes, constructing whole paintings by means of a network of interconnected brushmarks.

Obviously different brushes make different marks, so try to discover their capabilities by practising "drawing" with a brush. You can make a wide range of marks with just one brush if you vary the way you hold it and the amount of pressure you apply. Most people tend to hold a brush as though they were writing, gripping it firmly near the ferrule, but, although this gives maximum control, it can limit the artist's expressive style. Try holding it nearer the top and varying the pressure from heavy to light, flicking it at the end of a stroke. See what happens if you use a flat brush and twist it in mid-stroke, or draw out a brushstroke as far as you can so that the brush is progressively starved of paint. This kind of doodling is never a waste of time, as you will be training your hand, albeit unconsciously.

Drawing with paint

1 *The artist has chosen to work on a smooth-surfaced watercolour paper, which enables her to combine strong brushmarks with softer wet-into-wet painting. She begins with broad strokes, letting the colours run together slightly.*

2 *The first applications of paint have now begun to dry, but are still damp enough for the next brushstrokes to spread slightly and soften.*

3 *Crisp strokes of almost undiluted colour are now worked wet on dry over the softer brushmarks. Notice the position of the brush; instead of pulling it downwards in the usual way, the artist uses an upward flick.*

5 *A broader effect suggesting the dark green foliage is produced by flooding dark green paint into lighter green, in a modified wet-into-wet technique.*

4 (Above) *At the top of the picture, the succession of criss-crossing brushmarks, where the first colours show through the later ones, creates a lively impression of light and movement.*

6 (Below) *The small backrun at the top of the tree and the jagged edges on the tree trunk and foliage formed as the washes dried out; these are typical semi-accidents which occur during watercolour work. Experienced painters exploit such effects rather than trying to correct them, and here they enhance the lively, edgy quality of the picture.*

As we have seen earlier, highlights in watercolour are normally created by painting around them. There is, however, another method, which involves putting on paint and then removing it. Highlights made by the classic reserving method have crisp, clear edges, but often a softer, more diffuse effect is required. For example, clouds or matt-surfaced objects do not have sharp highlights and would look unrealistic if painted in this way. In such cases, lifting out is the method you need.

It is beautifully easy; all you do is lay down the paint and, before it has dried, dab into it or wipe it with a very slightly damp sponge, a rag, a piece of kitchen paper or blotting paper – anything absorbent in fact. If you have ever worried about how to create the effect of white clouds in a blue sky without laboriously painting around the shapes (which looks unnatural anyway), your problems are solved. Simply lay a gradated wash and then dab into it or, for windclouds, sweep across the paper with your chosen implement. More complex colour effects can be created by lifting out one colour to reveal another. For the soft dappling of foliage, for example, you could lay a dark green wash over a lighter one which has been allowed to dry, then lift out some of the darker colour.

Small, soft highlights, such as those on matt-surfaced objects or on distant water in a landscape, can be made by allowing a cotton bud (swab) or virtually dry paintbrush to suck up some of the colour where you want the highlight to be. You can even lift out dry paint in small areas, using a firmer pressure and slightly more water. Alternatively, you can scrape into the paint with a blade. This scratching technique is commonly used for tiny, fine lines, such as those created by light on blades of grass.

Lifting out clouds

1 *Having laid a pale blue wash, allowed it to dry and then painted a multi-coloured wash on top, the artist uses a crumpled piece of kitchen paper to dab into wet paint.*

2 *To darken the undersides of the clouds, more colour has been laid on, wet into wet, and is partially removed again with kitchen paper.*

3 *The effect is very realistic and has been achieved with the minimum of time and effort. The soft clouds at the top contrast with the irregular edges formed when the darker washes dried out.*

Lifting out dry paint

2 (Right) *A cotton bud (swab) dipped into water is now used to work into the green paint, creating much softer highlights than can be achieved by reserving.*

1 *A series of green washes has been painted over a dry yellow one, with small areas of the yellow reserved for the sharper highlights.*

3 *Finally, tiny highlights are made by scratching into the dry paint with a scalpel blade. This must always be done at a final stage in the painting because it breaks up the paper surface, making it impossible to lay colour on top.*

4 (Right) *The lifting-out method is ideal for the soft, diffused highlights seen on foliage or matt-surfaced objects, but is most effective when contrasted with the crisper edges achieved by reserving areas of the painting.*

MASKING

Reserving highlights by painting around them is ideal if the required shape is reasonably large and clearly defined, but often the highlights may be small and intricate, in which case it is helpful to use masking fluid. Some watercolourists disdain the use of such methods, regarding them as "mechanical" or "tricksy", but others find them indispensable.

The great advantage of masking is that it removes the worry and allows you to paint more freely. If you have to think constantly about not taking the paint over little shapes which you want to reserve, there is a danger that your work may become tight and fussy; masking fluid allows you to work as broadly and splashily as you like, knowing that those areas are protected.

Masking fluid is a viscous solution sold in small bottles. It is either white or yellow, the latter being the best choice because you can see where you are putting it on. It is applied with a brush and, when dry, washes are laid on top. When these too are dry, the fluid is removed by rubbing with a finger or a plastic eraser. Wash the brush immediately because, once dry, the fluid is very difficult to remove from the hairs – and don't use your most expensive brush.

Highlights with masking fluid

1 *Here the artist is using masking fluid to reserve small areas suggesting dappled light. She starts with a pencil drawing and then paints on the masking fluid with a small brush.*

Painting white shapes
Masking fluid not only provides a convenient means of reserving white paper for highlights, but can also be used in a more positive way to make distinctive brushmarks of white. Being thick, it holds the marks of the brush very effectively, as you can see from these examples, where the fluid was removed after the paint had dried. You are thus virtually painting with white, in a way that is otherwise impossible with watercolour alone.

2 A light blue-grey wash is taken over the whole
  area of tree trunks and foliage and allowed to dry
before further greens and yellows are painted, largely
wet into wet.

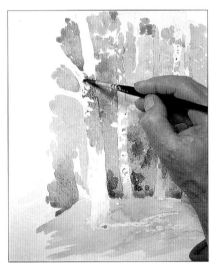

3 The colours of the foliage must be kept separate
  from those of the tree trunks, so the first colours
were dried with a hairdryer. Browns are now painted
over the masking fluid.

4 (Right) The fluid is removed by rubbing with a
  finger. The paint must be perfectly dry before this
is done, so again a hairdryer was used.

5 (Above) When the
  masking fluid is
taken off, you often find
that some of the white
highlights are too stark.
In this case they have
been left as white on
the two left-hand tree
trunks, but slightly
darkened elsewhere;
light yellow washes were
laid over the leaves in the
centre and on the lighter
patch of foreground.

USING OPAQUE PAINT

Watercolour has not always been used as a transparent medium in the past, nor is it always used as one today. Artists such as Albrecht Dürer in the Renaissance period and J.M.W. Turner in the 19th century used watercolour which was similar to today's gouache paints. Many of today's artists use gouache and watercolour together, or mix their colours with a little opaque white, which gives them body while still preserving much of their translucent quality (opaque watercolour is sometimes referred to as "body colour").

Opaque paint, like masking fluid, is frowned upon by some purists, who regard it as cheating, but this is nonsense. The point of painting is to exploit your medium to the full, to gain the effects you want; if you can do this by adding opaque white, then go ahead and do it. It is the perfect method for atmospheric weather effects, for example, such as cloud-shrouded hills or the soft lights on water.

You can add an extra dimension to your work by using coloured paper, whether or not you are adding white to the paint. Working over a base colour gives you a start in the process of building up the colours; it is particularly well suited to any paintings which are to be relatively dark overall, without bright highlights. It is now possible to buy coloured watercolour papers, but they are not easily available, so you might consider trying some of the papers made for pastel work, which come in an extensive colour range. Stretch them first, however, as they are thinner than most watercolour papers.

Working on tinted paper

1 *The artist is using a paper whose surface is rather similar to the Ingres paper used for pastel work, but it is thicker and does not buckle when wet. He makes a careful drawing of the buildings within the landscape before putting on any colour.*

2 *The secret behind an effective opaque-watercolour technique is to add white to the paint only where necessary, and to use it sparingly. Here white has been used for the sky, but the darker paint now being applied is pure watercolour.*

3 *For the houses, white with a small addition of crimson is painted into pure white, wet into wet, to create a slight blending of colours. Wet-into-wet effects are less dramatic and unpredictable with opaque paint, because it runs less freely.*

4 *Again opaque white is mixed with watercolour, as it was for the roofs of the houses. The white used is gouache paint, which the artist finds more satisfactory than the Chinese white sold for watercolour work.*

5 *In the final stages, a small brush was used to outline the roofs and paint in details of windows; now the foreground foliage is built up with small washes and overlaid brushstrokes of pure watercolour. The darker colours have been kept transparent throughout.*

6 *(Above) The finished picture is delightfully delicate and fresh, retaining the translucent qualities associated with watercolour. The colour of the paper, deliberately left to show between brushstrokes in the background and foreground, plays an important part in the overall colour scheme.*

TEXTURING METHODS

It can be hard to know where to start when describing texture in a fluid medium like watercolour. How, for instance, do you give the impression of a shingle beach or a cornfield without painting every pebble or cornhead? In fact there are a good many special techniques to hand. One is dry brush which, as its name implies, means working with the minimum of paint on the brush so that it only partially covers the paper. This method is often used for grass, the hazy effect of distant trees or the fur of animals. The best brush to use is a flat one, with the hairs slightly splayed out between thumb and forefinger and then dabbed onto blotting paper or absorbent kitchen paper to remove the excess paint.

Another popular method is spattering or flicking paint onto the paper with an old toothbrush. The toothbrush is loaded with colour and held above the work; the handle

Dry-brushed grasses

1 *As the name of the method implies, the brush must be fairly dry so, after dipping it into the paint, the artist dabs it onto a piece of kitchen paper to remove the surplus paint.*

2 *Using a square-ended brush, she splays the hairs out slightly and then gently drags the brush over the paper, creating a series of fine lines.*

3 *(Left) One layer of dry brushing has been laid over another to suggest the different directions in which the marsh grasses lean.*

Toothbrush spatter

1 A toothbrush is loaded with paint, and a pencil is pulled across the bristles to release a fine spray.

2 The spatter is fairly close in tone to the underlying wash and avoids being too obtrusive – it is easy to overdo this method.

Paintbrush spatter

1 This time dark paint is spattered into a light green wash using a bristle brush tapped against a pencil, producing larger droplets.

2 As the spattering was done wet into wet, the darker colour has spread out and blended to some extent with the lighter one.

of a brush, a knife or your thumbnail is drawn quickly across it to release a spray of droplets. This technique is very effective for suggesting texture without describing it too literally, but it should not be overdone, nor should it look too obtrusive. If you are spattering over a pale wash, perhaps for a sandy beach, don't make the spattered colour too dark or it will look artificial. Spattering can also be used in a purely decorative way, to create an area of colour with a stippled appearance.

A particularly exciting method, ideal for the texture of old pitted rocks or crumbling walls, is salt spatter, which involves dropping crystals of coarse sea salt into wet paint. The salt granules absorb the water while "pushing away" the pigment, leaving a pattern of pale, crystalline shapes when they are removed. The effects vary according to how wet the paint is and which colours you use – some pigments are "heavier" than others and do not move so readily. For the best results, apply the salt just after the wash has lost its sheen, which indicates that it is beginning to dry. The salt itself takes a long time to dry, but it is worth persevering with the technique.

Salt spatter

1 This technique works best on a non-absorbent paper, and here smooth (hot-pressed) watercolour paper is used. The salt is dropped into a wash and begins to absorb the water immediately.

2 (Right) These examples show some of the different effects which can be achieved; they vary according to the colour used, the wetness of the wash and the closeness of the crystals.

WAX RESIST

In one way this technique is similar to that of using masking fluid. Both involve creating a block which prevents the paint from reaching the paper, but wax resist gives a very different effect. It is based on the mutual antipathy of oil (the wax) and water (the paint). If you scribble over paper with a household candle or wax crayon and then apply washes, the paint will slide off the wax. Unlike masking fluid, however, which leaves perfect shapes when removed, the wax creates a subtler, lightly speckled effect. This is because watercolour paper is textured, so the wax adheres only to the top of the grain, unless you draw very heavily indeed with the candle or crayon.

Wax resist is a simple technique which can yield quite beautiful results. It is often used in landscape, for skies lightly broken by clouds or the gentle gleam of water on lakes, rivers and seas. It also provides yet another way of describing texture. The roughened surface of an old building, a crumbling cliff or an ancient gnarled tree, for example, can be quickly and easily suggested with a light application of wax under loose wet-into-wet washes.

If you want a coloured resist, you can use wax-oil crayons or the new oil bars, which serve the purpose very well. You can make the wax underdrawing as simple or as complex as you like. Some artists build up paintings in layers, applying crayon, then paint and then more crayon, sometimes even scratching into the wax before putting on more paint. It is an exciting method to try as it contains an element of surprise – you never quite know what will happen.

Watercolour and oil bar

1 *This artist uses wax resist a good deal in her work, building up effects by means of a layering technique. She has begun with loose watercolour washes and now scribbles over the dry paint with a transparent oil bar.*

Types of wax

The final results depend on the texture of the paper, the pressure applied and the kind of wax used. A household candle was used for the first example and an oil bar for the other two. More delicate lines can be made with a wax-oil crayon.

2 As the watercolour is applied on top, it slides off the wax, leaving small blobs and speckles. This method is often used to suggest texture.

3 A further application of oil bar has been followed by another watercolour wash, which is smeared down the paper to create an effect of brushstrokes.

4 While the paint in the foreground is still wet, a craft knife is used to scratch into both wax and paint. Dark lines are created where the wax is removed, as the paint seeps into the slightly scuffed paper surface.

5 A lighter scratching method is used for the sky, but in this case the effect is different because the knife removes the layer of watercolour on top of the wax, leaving white marks.

6 (Right) The artist has not attempted a precise representation of the landscape features; the wax resist in the foreground suggests water without describing it literally. Her approach is impressionistic and, to a large extent, she allows the painting itself to dictate her procedure.

LINE & WASH

This technique, which combines drawing and painting, has been in use for a long time, but has lost none of its appeal. Traditionally it was employed by illustrators – as it still is today – as a means of introducing colour into what were basically drawings, usually in pen and ink. Nowadays artists exploit the technique of line and wash in more personal and often highly inventive ways.

Line and wash is essentially a mixed-media technique and, as in all such work, it is important to try to integrate the two media to create a unified image. Thus it is not always wise to begin with the drawing, or at any rate to take the drawing to a finished stage, before putting on colour. Generally the best and most "painterly" effects are created by developing the two side by side, adding more colour and more line as the picture demands.

You don't have to use pen for line and wash – watercolour is often combined with pencil drawing, the pencil lines providing detail and touches of definition. Pencil and watercolour marry very well together, as pencil gives a gentler and less assertive line than pen.

However, on the whole, pen is the implement most often used, so if you want to try this technique you will need to experiment with different pens, of which there is a bewilderingly large range on the market. You can use fine fibre-tipped and felt-tipped pens (but make sure they are non-fading), fountain pens or dip pens. For the beginner, the latter are probably the best, as a holder with interchangeable nibs is relatively inexpensive. Waterproof ink is normally used, but it is worth trying water-soluble ink too. This runs slightly when the watercolour washes are laid on top, which can be an effective way of softening the line.

Pen and watercolour

1 *The artist likes to develop line and colour together, so he has begun by making a pencil drawing to provide some guidelines for the first washes, which he applies loosely, wet into wet.*

2 *With the washes now dry, he draws with a pen, using waterproof ink. He keeps the line drawing to a minimum at this stage of the work.*

3 *The drawing has been considerably strengthened with bold lines and areas of hatching and cross-hatching. To avoid giving too much prominence to the linear element, the artist now applies darker colour.*

6 (Above) *When the entire drawing is done at the beginning, pen-and-wash work can become rather tight and fussy, giving the effect of a "filled-in drawing". The artist has avoided this pitfall and integrated the drawing and painting media, while still providing a good contrast between linearity and boldly applied colour.*

4 *The area in front of the house is defined with further pen work. Notice how the wet-into-wet washes in the foreground have dried with hard, irregular edges, complementing the pen lines.*

5 *A succession of washes has been laid over the large tree, again with the paint used loosely and freely; final touches are added with a finer nib than that used previously.*

BACKRUNS

If you have ever tried to work into a wash before it is dry, you may have come across the phenomenon of the backrun. The new paint seeps into the old, creating an odd blotch with hard, jagged edges – some people call it a cauliflower for obvious reasons. Normally backruns cause alarm and despondency because you may have to abandon a whole piece of paper, or at least wash the area down with a sponge and begin again.

However, a very important part of watercolour work is learning how to exploit accidental effects of this nature – watercolours are never totally predictable. Some artists induce backruns deliberately, or simply allow them to happen and then leave them alone because they improve the painting. The effects they create are quite different from those made by more conventional means, and the strange shapes are often highly suggestive. For example, a backrun in a sky can often look like a cloud, possibly suggesting a different treatment

from the one you originally had in mind, while one in the foreground might provide the perfect touch of additional interest. In flower painting, backruns are particularly useful, often resembling the shapes of petals and flowers.

WATERCOLOUR PALETTE

WATERCOLOUR PANS

Backruns cannot be controlled with much precision, but you are not altogether at the mercy of events. You can make them happen at will if you always use paint which has a higher water content than the original colour (thick paint on thin will not work). You can tilt the board, as in any wet-into-wet work, and then use a hairdryer to "stop" the run when you are satisfied with the effect, but remember that wet-into-wet paint goes on moving until it dries.

Accidental backruns

These examples show what can happen when you panic and try to work back into a wash. In the first, the wash was very wet; in the second, it appeared dry but was not.

Deliberate backruns

1 A dark indigo wash is laid first, and a slightly
more watery solution of alizarin crimson is
then dropped into the wet paint. It begins to
spread immediately.

2 The paint will continue to move until it is fully
dry. At this stage the first wash has begun to dry
at the edges, but the central area is still wet, and the
crimson continues to bleed into the darker colour.

3 Yellow is now dropped into the centre; this in
turn pushes the crimson away to create a pale
area within the darker colours.

4 (Right) Finally the paper is allowed to dry out
and a light crimson applied wet on dry, followed
by a darker crimson worked wet into wet. A variety of
flower-like effects can be produced in this way.

47

PAINT ADDITIVES

The pigment used to make watercolours is bound with a gum called gum arabic, which can also be used as a painting medium; it is sold in most good art shops. A little gum mixed with water (known as gum water) makes the paint more lustrous and less runny, giving it extra body. This allows you to build up an area of the picture in small separate brushstrokes which do not merge together. It is thus useful for any area of a picture where you want a lot of precise detail, particularly if you intend to use dark colours, which can otherwise become muddy and dull. It is also useful for lifting out dry paint. If you lay a colour mixed with gum water over another paler wash and let it dry before working into areas with a wet brush, the top layer of paint will come away very easily because the water dissolves the gum, revealing the paint beneath.

Using gum water

1 *The artist began with conventional water and paint washes, and has painted the trees with dark green paint mixed with gum water (about two parts of water to one of gum). Notice the richness of the colours and how each brushstroke remains separate.*

2 *Gum arabic also facilitates the lifting-out technique. The gum is water-soluble, so a wet brush dabbed into the paint removes the top layer.*

3 *A damp rag is dabbed lightly into the paint to create softer, more diffuse highlights. Note how the original yellow wash remains intact; this is because gum water was not used for the first colours.*

4 (Left) *You may find that gum water adds an extra dimension to your work; the effect of the lifted-out highlights is unlike anything achieved by standard methods. The artist herself, who had never used the technique before, was delighted.*

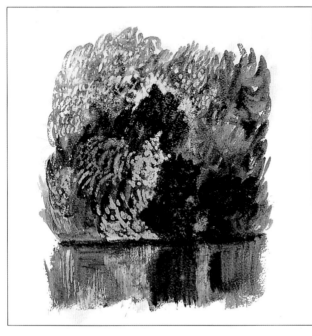

Mixing paint with soap

1 *The brush has been dipped into a strong solution of colour and rubbed over a bar of soap. This thickens the paint so that it holds the marks of the brush without sacrificing the transparency of the colour.*

2 *A bristle brush gives a different effect because the soapy paint can be used more thickly, in swirling strokes so that it forms ridges and bubbles. These remain when the paint has dried, creating an intriguing impression of specks and small circles.*

Watercolour and turpentine

1 *The brush has been dipped first into turpentine and then into paint, thus creating a striated effect as the paint withdraws from the oily substance of the turpentine.*

2 *Here turpentine has been scrubbed over the whole surface of the paper with a bristle brush before paint is applied on top.*

3 *The same method has been used for this example, but the brushstrokes are not as close together, having been drawn out to produce a light, scratchy texture.*

4 *In this case turpentine has been dropped into a wet wash; the water-and-paint mixture is then pushed outwards to form a pale shape.*

Ox gall, another medium sold specially for watercolour work, has the opposite effect. This makes the paint flow more freely and is therefore known as a "water-tension breaker".

So much for the conventional additives. There are some interesting "alternative" ones too, such as soap. This has a similar effect to gum arabic, thickening the paint so that it holds the marks of the brush, but with an added dimension – the bubbles, which form as you work, leave intriguing rings and blobs when dry. Soap is particularly useful for creating texture

effects and could be ideal for a dramatic stormy sky.

You can also create interesting effects in watercolour by exploiting a variation of the wax-resist technique. In this case turpentine is used which, being an oily substance, repels the watercolour. If you lay down some turpentine and then paint over it, the paint and the oil will separate, but only partially, giving a streaky or marbled appearance. Alternatively you can mix up some paint and dip your brush into turpentine before applying it. Like all such methods, this one is unpredictable but fun to try.

COMPARATIVE DEMONSTRATION

Non-professional watercolour painters sometimes restrict themselves unnecessarily by following, or studying under, one particular artist, trying to paint in exactly the same style. This can be valuable – artists have always been influenced by their teachers or by artists of the past whom they admire – but it can mislead you into thinking that there is only one way of doing things and that certain techniques are somehow wrong. To show that no two people work in the same way, we have asked two different artists to paint the same subject using their preferred method.

John Lidzey uses a combination of wet-into-wet and wet-on-dry methods, painting on smooth (hot-pressed) paper, because he likes to encourage the colours to run into each other and to form pools and backruns. Rosalind Cuthbert, on the other hand, paints on medium (Not surface) paper, using the classic wet-on-dry technique.

(Above) *An attractive still life of blue glass and silver objects is assembled on a checked tablecloth.*

Watercolour on smooth paper

1 *To make it easier to judge the colours needed for the silver bowl, the artist begins by laying light washes over the background. A careful pencil drawing was made first in order to keep these early washes away from the edges of the objects.*

2 *For the main body of the vase, a soft effect has been created by painting wet into wet, but the white highlights must be sharply defined, so these have been reserved by painting carefully around them. Parts of this orange-yellow wash will in turn be reserved as highlights, together with the small patch on the right, which has been left white.*

3 *The artist's method is to use wet-into-wet techniques only for certain areas of the painting; both here and on the silver pot he produces clean, clear edges by working wet on dry, drying the picture with a hairdryer between each stage.*

4 A darker wash laid on the apple is dabbed with cotton wool (a cotton ball) to create a softly diffused highlight. Cotton wool (cotton balls) and a hairdryer are both important items in the artist's "tool-kit".

5 The background colour is taken carefully around the edges of the glass. Although the glass and vase have been painted mainly wet into wet – you can see the effect clearly in this photograph – the painting has been dried to prevent the new colour from bleeding into the blue.

6 To soften areas of the background and provide a slight variation in tone and colour, damp cotton wool (a cotton ball) is again employed to lift out some of the wet paint. Granulation, one of the attractive accidental effects which watercolourists like to exploit, often occurs on smooth paper.

7 Here you can see how the original wash laid on the apple in Step 2 has been reserved for highlight effects, with the darker colours painted over it wet on dry. The added dark shadow gives the apple extra solidity.

8 The combination of soft, wet-into-wet effects and crisp, clean edges is very attractive. The treatment of the silver bowl and the top of the vase shows the importance of a preliminary drawing in watercolour work; each highlight and patch of reflected colour must be precisely placed, in order to explain the forms of the objects.

Continued ▷

W
A
T
E
R
C
O
L
O
U
R

1 *As in the previous demonstration, the artist has begun with an underdrawing, although here the lines are lighter. Unlike the other artist, she does not begin with the background, but establishes the colours of the glass and vase immediately.*

2 *(Above) As blue is the dominant colour in the painting, no other colours have yet been introduced. Two main blues have been used – ultramarine for the vase and Winsor (phthalocyanine) blue, a cooler, greener colour, for the glass and cloth.*

3 *The artist plans to key the background and foreground colours to those of the vase and bottle, therefore she concentrates on these first. The dark ultramarine now being used has also been laid over much of the glass, with some of the lighter blues reserved for highlights.*

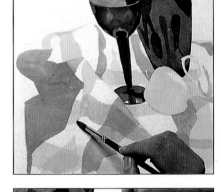

4 *(Right) Light yellow washes are laid on the cloth and apple and, where the yellow is painted over the light blue, the two colours mix to produce green. A warmer, more orangey yellow has been painted over the blue at the bottom of the vase, which reflects colour from the apple.*

5 *By completing the vase before the other objects, the artist is able to evaluate the strength of the colours needed for the apple and its reflection in the silver bowl, which she paints next.*

6 *(Right) The broken colour of the apple and the inside of the silver bowl have been achieved by stippling, a version of the dry-brush technique, which is used once more for this shadow. Taking up the minimum of paint with the brush, the artist dabs it lightly onto the paper.*

9 In the final stages, a few further light washes were laid on the tablecloth to strengthen it slightly, and the area of background behind the table was darkened with a warm blue-grey. This is the one area of the painting in which colours were blended wet into wet, to achieve the required soft effect.

7 Leaving the background until last is often a good idea in still-life painting, as sometimes you do not know what kind of background is needed until the objects have been painted. Here a yellow similar to that of the cloth is chosen; the board is turned upside-down to facilitate the laying of the wash.

8 To give objects such as the blue glass extra definition and impact, fine highlights are added where edges catch the light.

LANDSCAPE

In most people's minds, watercolour is perhaps more closely associated with landscape than with any other subject. This may be because there is a long tradition of sketching in watercolour but, whatever the reason, there is no doubt that the fluidity and brilliance of watercolour, together with its portability, make it an excellent medium for on-the-spot painting.

Of course, you don't have to work directly from life all the time – we will be looking at alternative methods later on. If you are interested in landscape, however, it is advisable to do at least some location work, as there is no substitute for a direct response to your subject. Before you begin to translate your response into paint, you must make some initial decisions about how you are going to organize your picture in terms of composition.

Unity and contrast
In the landscape shown below, Juliette Palmer has created visual links between the sky and the land areas by using similar shapes for both the small clouds and the trees. This has given an overall unity to her composition, with the straight lines of the houses providing contrast. In The Conservatory *(left) she has exploited this kind of contrast more thoroughly, using the geometric shapes and light colours of the architectural features as a foil for the free forms and bright colours of the flowers.*

Placing a focal point
(Left) If there is one particular feature in your chosen view which catches your attention, such as a dark tree against a light background or a vivid area of colour, it will become the focal point in your painting, and you must decide where to place it and how to emphasize it. In Juliette Palmer's Peak District – Springtime *the focal point (the white house) has been placed slightly off-centre, and the eye is led towards it by the curving diagonals of the foreground field and wall and the strong shape of the tall tree*

Making visual links

(Above) *Foregrounds are a frequent cause of failure in landscape composition; often they are treated in more detail than the middle distance and distance, making the picture look disconnected. In* From the Mule Path with Fig *Joan Elliott Bates has treated the foreground with the minimum of definition, but has taken care to link the fig tree to the rest of the picture both by letting the branches overlap the buildings and by using similar curving lines for the hills beyond.*

MAKING THE PICTURE

Even though you are simply painting what you can see, you still need to compose your picture. This doesn't mean that you have to move trees around or invent shadows where there are none, but you do have to decide what viewpoint to take, which part of the scene to concentrate on, how much of the picture you will devote to foreground and so on. Before you start, walk around a bit to find the position that gives you the most interesting angle on the subject; once you have chosen the viewpoint you are halfway to composing the picture.

However, you still need to decide where to place the horizon and to consider whether there are any elements in the scene which you can emphasize for effect, or any which you can play down or perhaps leave out altogether. You are not copying the

Creating movement

(Right) *A good landscape painting should encourage the viewer's eye to travel into and around the scene, to create movement in the composition. In* Road to Ronda *Pip Carpenter has achieved this quality both through her energetic brushwork and the way she has organized the picture. The area of trees and barely defined grass on the left leads towards the curving path, which the eye naturally follows. Paths, roads, streams or rivers leading from foreground to back ground are common compositional devices.*

scene; you are making your own statement about it and you don't have to include everything you see. After all, you would hardly try to paint every blade of grass in the foreground – you would generalize to create an impression of grass. So if there is a small, featureless shrub in the foreground which obscures your view of a grand tree further back, ignore it; alternatively, move your position so that it is less obtrusive.

The golden rule of composition is to avoid symmetry. It is never wise to divide your picture into halves, with the horizon exactly in the middle, particularly if it is a flat horizon line, as in a seascape. Nor should you place the most important element in the painting, for example a tree, right in the middle. Symmetry is dull and static and you should aim for a feeling of life and movement in your work.

KEEPING UP WITH THE LIGHT

Changing light is a constant problem for those who work out of doors. Even if the sun does not actually go in, thus removing all the shadows and much of the colour from the scene, it moves inexorably round the sky, altering the direction of the shadows and shining first on one side of a tree and then on the other.

The only way to cope with this is to work as fast as possible without actually rushing; restrict yourself to a fairly small scale so that you can cover the paper as quickly as possible. It is helpful to make a note of the direction of the light as soon as you begin. Either put a small pencil cross in a corner of the picture or block in the main shadows first – in this way, you won't be tempted to change them.

Do not try to work on the same painting over a whole day, unless it is overcast, because the scene you saw in the morning will be quite different from the one you see in the evening. It is better either to give yourself a definite time limit – say three hours – or to work on two consecutive days at the same time. Experienced painters can

Human interest
(Left) *You can often give additional interest to a landscape, or stress a centre of interest, by including one or two figures. In Ronald Jesty's* A Wild Day, *the men shielding their heads against the spray from the breaking wave and the woman pointing her hand in warning introduce an element of narrative, and both these and the surrounding dark rocks provide contrasts of tone which draw attention to the picture's focal point.*

often continue in the face of changing conditions, but only because they have well-trained visual memories and are sufficiently disciplined to stick to what they originally saw.

WORKING INDOORS

It is not really practical to paint big pictures out of doors, but a good method is to make a series of drawings and small colour sketches on location, then to compose and paint the actual picture indoors. This has the dual advantage of giving you direct experience of the subject and allowing you to paint at your own pace, incorporating any special techniques which you feel might improve the picture.

Making sketches for a painting, as opposed to simply sketching for the fun of it, is rather a special skill, as you must learn to give yourself sufficient visual information from which to work. Artists often make written notes about colours, shapes and so on in their sketchbooks, to help jog their memories when they are recreating a scene

later. Even when making colour sketches, try to back these up with suggestions to yourself – it is better to have too much information than too little.

You can also use photographs as a basis for painting. You may have been told that you should never work from photographs, but this is not realistic. Most painters have limited time at their disposal and the weather often makes outdoor work impossible, so it is better to paint from photographs than not to paint at all.

There are problems, however. The camera is seldom reliable over colour; it loses many subtle nuances and often reduces dark colours to a formless mass with no detail. Photographs also tend to flatten out perspective and reduce the feeling of three-dimensional space.

To give themselves a wider choice of possibilities, artists who use photographs usually take several versions of the subject, which they can then combine in their own composition. Sometimes they make sketches as well.

Studio paintings
(Above) *Patrick Cullen paints large-scale watercolours in the studio from sketches: this painting,* Landscape in La Crete Region, Tuscany, *is over five feet wide. Referring to sketches and drawings done on the spot, and sometimes making a working drawing to plan the composition, he paints area by area, building up deep, rich colours with a series of overlaid brushstrokes and occasionally washing down the paint to achieve soft gradations of tone and colour.*

DEMONSTRATION

Hazel Soan is known primarily as a watercolour landscape painter, although she does work in oils on occasion. She likes to paint on the spot whenever possible but, if time does not permit this, she composes her paintings in the studio, making extensive use of photographic reference. She seldom works from just one photograph, but uses a combination of several, selecting different elements from each and editing out unwanted features. The photographs are put away when she has reached a certain stage of work so that the painting can develop independently.

COLOURS
USED *mauve, permanent rose, cobalt blue, cerulean blue, ultramarine, yellow ochre, cadmium yellow, new gamboge, Winsor green, burnt sienna and a tiny amount of cadmium red*

1 *The artist generally uses masking fluid to reserve highlight areas; here she begins to paint it in, referring to the photograph and guided by her initial light pencil drawing.*

2 *She builds up gradually from light washes to darker ones in the classic watercolour technique, working mainly wet on dry but using wet-into-wet methods in certain areas. A light rose pink and mauve mixture is laid over the masking fluid on the left of the picture to be rubbed into later on.*

3 *The colours of the flowers and the vivid red-brown of the foreground set the key for the overall warm colour scheme, so these are blocked in at an early stage.*

5 With the distant trees now complete, the artist turns her attention to the area on the far side of the lake. Here the colours are stronger but, for a relatively soft effect, the wet colours are blotted lightly so that they are not so saturated.

4 After about an hour's work, the main colours have been established, to be darkened and strengthened in places with further washes. The wet-into-wet method has so far been used only in the background, where soft effects are appropriate.

6 To strengthen the foreground, a dark mixture is painted over the light pink and red-brown washes. This area is worked wet on dry to achieve crisp edges, giving the foreground a sharper focus than the more distant parts of the landscape.

7 (Right) The masking fluid has been removed from some of the flowerheads, which are now touched in with pink. The fluid is removed at various stages during the painting, depending on how strong the highlights are to be.

Continued ▷

8 *The foliage of the large tree on the right had previously been painted wet into wet to give gentle blends of colour, with yellows merging into blue-greens. Crisp brushmarks now define those leaves nearer the foreground.*

9 *The masking fluid is removed from the flowerheads in the foreground by gently rubbing with a putty eraser. On the reeds it will be left in place, creating an attractive speckled texture similar to the effect of wax resist.*

10 *The flowers are now painted in yellow, with tiny patches of the white paper left uncovered. They could have been painted over the light blue of the water, without the use of masking fluid, but even the palest of underlying colours would have compromised the purity of this brilliant yellow.*

11 *Touches of deep pink are added to the flowerheads in the foreground of the picture.*

12 (Right) *In the final stages, the tonal contrasts in the foreground are strengthened to bring this area forward and increase the feeling of depth in the painting. The artist drops in dark colour wet into wet, using the tip of the brush.*

13 (Above) *The artist deliberated over whether to make more of the reflections, which were clearly visible in one of her photographs of the scene, but she decided against it, preferring to emphasize the triangular shape made by the pale expanse of water.*

FLOWERS

If landscape is the most popular subject for watercolour painters, flowers are not far behind. Sometimes, of course, the two subject areas overlap. When you are painting flowers in their natural habitat, perhaps in a garden or a park, you are painting a "mini-landscape", whereas flowers in a vase or bowl indoors become a floral still life.

Whether you paint flowers indoors or out (or both) is up to you, but for those who are new to flower painting it is perhaps best to avoid the problems of changing light, unreliable weather and discomfort. It demands concentration and patience to paint flowers. By setting up your own floral still life, you can take time to arrange it and then work at your own pace.

ARRANGING THE GROUP

Arranging any still-life group takes careful thought, and floral groups are no exception. First you must consider the balance of colours – in general you don't want too many different blooms, with all the shapes and colours fighting for attention. The most effective flower paintings are often those with one predominant colour. You could choose all white flowers, for example, or a selection of blue ones, perhaps with one yellow flower for contrast.

Choose a receptacle which suits the flowers, making them look neither cramped nor swamped. Aim for a natural look and avoid the kind of formal, official arrangement that you sometimes see in churches and public places. Let some of the flowers overlap; have some higher than others, some turned away and others facing you.

PUTTING IT ON PAPER

You will paint more confidently if you start with a good drawing, but, before you begin,

Keeping it simple

(Below) *The kind of elaborate groups beloved of florists do not always make the best paintings, so when you begin to arrange your flowers see if you can improve the composition by limiting their number. In Poppies Elisabeth Harden has given impact to the shapes and colours of the poppies by concentrating on a few flowerheads, including one or two small white flowers and seedheads for contrast. As the red against the dark green foliage in the foreground makes such a dramatic statement, she has wisely left the background unpainted.*

Flowers in still life

(Left) *Flowers do not have to be painted on their own; they can form part of a more general still life, as in* Still Life, Welsh Kitchen *by Joan Elliott Bates. The flowers are the main centre of interest, but the objects and curtain have been carefully arranged, as they play a subsidiary but vitally important role in the composition. Notice particularly the way the curtain sweeps around and upwards, creating a strong curve which provides a foil for the flowers and vase. This is a mixed-media painting, in which watercolour has been combined with Conté crayon and pastel.*

consider how to place the group of flowers on your paper. Again, try to avoid symmetry; don't place the vase exactly in the middle of the picture unless there is enough asymmetry in the arrangement itself to balance this. Decide how much of the group you are going to include. A device often used is "cropping", which means allowing one or two blooms and stems to go out of the picture at the top. This can be very effective if you are painting tall flowers, while a wider group could be cropped at one side or the other.

The foreground and background need consideration too. Avoid leaving a blank space on either side of the vase. Sometimes

this can be done by making a positive element out of the shadow cast by the vase; other alternatives are to put the vase on a patterned cloth or to take out one or two of the flowers and place them in front, to one side of the vase.

Backgrounds in watercolour flower painting are often left vague and undefined, but they don't have to be. If there is a window behind the group you could lightly suggest it, thus giving a geometric framework to the composition. Or you could set the group against a patterned wallpaper, which might echo and reinforce the pattern made by the flowers themselves. As a general rule, however, it is best to

Colour unity

(Above) *In* Daffodils and Fruit *Elisabeth Harden has paid attention to the colour schemes, ensuring that links are established between the flowers and objects. The lemon and grapefruit echo the yellows of the daffodils, and similar blues and greys appear in the vase, cup and saucer, and tablecloth. The muted greens of the leaves give greater prominence to the whites, yellows and greys.*

Making a pattern
(Left) *There is a strong built-in pattern element in floral subjects, which has been exploited to the full in Audrey Macleod's* Casablanca Lilies. *Although the forms of the flowers and leaves have been built up carefully so that they are completely realistic and three-dimensional, the painting makes its initial impact as a pattern of light on dark. The soft effects on the leaves and in parts of the background were achieved by washing down the paint.*

avoid too much detail in the background or foreground – the flowers are the centre of interest in the painting, and, by introducing too many other elements, you could rob them of their importance.

THE PAINTING

The essence of flower painting is lightness of touch; if you overwork the paint the freshness of the colours will be lost. Try to work broadly and freely, at least initially, blocking in the main shapes and colours and reserving detail for the final stages. Masking fluid can help you here. If you are painting white or light-coloured flowers against a mass of green foliage, you can mask the flowers and leave them until a later stage in the painting.

Try to set up contrasts between hard and soft edges, using the wet-into-wet technique in some places and painting wet on dry in others to form crisper areas (perhaps for certain well-defined petals or leaves). Don't be tempted to put in small details until you are sure that all the shapes and colours are working as they should – only in the final stages should you bring your tiny, fine brush into play.

Single blooms
(Above) *Although flowers are more generally painted as an arrangement in a vase, individual flowers make equally rewarding subjects. The artists of China and Japan brought flower painting of this kind to a high art, and Vicky Lowe's lovely* Sunflower *owes much to the Oriental tradition, both in the composition and in the technique, with each petal described by one swift, sure brushstroke. The soft effect where the dark centre of the flower merges into the petals has been achieved by dampening selected areas and dropping in wet paint.*

Using colour
(Opposite) *The way you treat flowers, or any other subject, depends on what it is that particularly interests you. For Gerry Baptist, colour is all-important; in* Clandon Garden Flowers *he has made the most of the brilliant reds and yellows by contrasting them with cool blues, mauves and dark greens. He has also paid attention to the flower shapes, however, and the pansies in the foreground in particular are clearly recognizable.*

Foregrounds and backgrounds

(Right) *When painting a tall floral group it can be difficult to know what to do with the area below and beside the vase. In Elisabeth Harden's painting of poppies, Audrey Macleod's* Casablanca Lilies *and this watercolour-and-wax-resist painting,* Roses, *by Debra Manifold, the artists have solved the problem by cropping the vase at the bottom of the picture. Here, the way in which the flowers merge into the dark background is also important to the composition, with the dark shape seeming to push upwards away from the pale foreground area, almost like a firework exploding.*

DEMONSTRATION

John Lidzey works entirely in watercolour, enjoying the challenge of its unpredictable nature and the way it encourages the painting to develop in its own way. He paints mainly landscapes and lovely light-filled interiors, the latter often including still lifes and flower groups. He is self-taught and has evolved a highly personal style, at which he arrived through experiment rather than the study of any other artist's methods. He enjoys wet-into-wet effects, although he controls them carefully, and usually paints on smooth-surfaced (hot-pressed) paper to allow the paint to move around more freely.

COLOURS USED *yellow ochre, aureolin yellow, cadmium yellow, ultramarine, cadmium red, carmine, indigo, Payne's gray*

(Above) *To start with, the artist arranges some bright, contrasting flowers in a vase.*

1 *The artist begins with a detailed drawing in 4B pencil. He takes considerable care with this, measuring to check the relative proportions of flowers to vase and so on, and making small marks across the paper to establish key points.*

2 *The vase and the shadow beneath are painted wet into wet, with one colour dropped into another so that they merge and mingle. A piece of cotton wool (a cotton ball) is used to control the flow of the paint.*

3 *The initial applications of paint are allowed to dry slightly; darker colour is then painted on top and dabbed with cotton wool (a cotton ball) to create soft highlights.*

4 *It is unusual to begin with the darkest colour – darks are generally built up gradually. In this case, however, the artist wanted to establish the deep blue of the vase in order to assess the strength of colour needed for the leaves.*

5 *The painting is at approximately the halfway stage, with the darkest colours in place and the white flowers reserved as bare paper.*

6 *A good deal of the paper is to be left uncovered for the flowers, but they must be given sufficient detail to suggest their structure. A fine-pointed brush is used to touch in the blue-grey shadow.*

7 *Carnations have a very distinctive petal formation; only a few touches of darker paint over the original pink wash are needed to describe their forms and character. The artist is working wet on dry here, to achieve the necessary crisp edges and strong tonal contrasts.*

8 (Above) *Finally, the flowers and leaves are built up with further wet-on-dry work. The pencil marks on the white flowers have been deliberately left showing, to provide further suggestions of detail. The artist subsequently improves the composition by placing paper masks at top and bottom to cut down the rather featureless expanses of foreground and background; look back at Step 5 to see what a difference this makes.*

Oil & Acrylic

ABOUT OIL & ACRYLIC

O
I
L
&
A
C
R
Y
L
I
C

Oil paint, although often seen as the traditional painting medium, is in fact younger than watercolour – or at any rate than a form of watercolour. The tempera paints which preceded oil and were used for both panel paintings and frescoes (wall and ceiling paintings) were made from pigments suspended in water and mixed with some form of glue, usually either egg yoke or casein, made from the curd of milk.

The idea of binding pigment with oil is often credited to the Flemish painter Jan Van Eyck in the early 15th century, but it is probable that other artists had experimented with similar ideas. Whatever the origins of the medium, it rapidly became popular. Tempera was a difficult medium to use, and the potential of oil-bound pigment quickly became obvious.

In the early days of oil painting, the paint was in the main used thinly, rather as tempera had been, but the colours were much richer, achieved by a layering technique called glazing. The surface was smooth, with no brushmarks visible. Later on, however, artists began to use the medium with more appreciation for its inherent qualities, and the marks of the brush (and sometimes of the knife) became an important part of the finished picture. Rembrandt's paintings, for example, demonstrate a love for the paint itself and what it can do, while in the works of the Impressionists, the brushwork and manner of applying the paint are inseparable from the subject matter.

OIL PAINTS TODAY

A walk round an exhibition of oil paintings instantly reveals the versatility of the medium, and it is this quality which has made it so popular from its inception to the

DAVID CURTIS
RED LANE,
NEAR DRONFIELD
(Left) *Brushwork is an important element in this oil painting on canvas; the brushstrokes follow the direction of the tree trunks and branches, describing them with great economy of means. Depth and recession are suggested by the contrast between thick and thin paint: on the right-hand tree the paint is thick and juicy, while for the area of blue distance it has been brushed lightly over the surface.*

GERRY BAPTIST PINES ON BEAUVBALLA
(Below) *This painting is also acrylic on canvas, but here the paint is slightly diluted with water to a consistency similar to that of gouache paint. The artist controls the juxtapositions of colour carefully, using complementaries such as yellow and mauve to create maximum impact while giving a realistic account of the landscape.*

TED GOULD
SNOW SCENE
(Above) *While David Curtis has juxtaposed warm golden browns with the blues and greys of the snow, the colour scheme in this painting is cool throughout; the yellow of the hat and scarf provides the only touch of contrast for the blues, blue-greens, greys and grey-browns. The painting is in acrylic, used thickly on canvas. This artist works mainly in oil, and applies the same methods to his acrylic work.*

PATRICK CULLEN CHURCH, SAN DONNINO
(Above) *Some artists like to paint on a coloured ground, but when the paint is used thinly, as in this lyrical oil painting, the white of the canvas reflects back through the colours to give a luminosity more often associated with watercolour.*

BRIAN BENNETT
MALVERN HILLS
(Left) *This artist, well known for his sensitive portrayals of the English countryside, works in the traditional medium of oil paint on canvas but, instead of the usual brushes, he uses painting knives, which he has "customized" to create particular effects. Knife painting can achieve bold, dramatic effects, but also surprisingly delicate ones, as can be seen in this painting.*

present day. Any painting medium should be seen as the servant of the artist, and oil paints behave in such an obedient manner that no two artists need paint in the same way. Oils can be used thinly or thickly, applied with knives or brushes – or even your fingers – and you can work on a large or a small scale. You can also move paint around on the picture surface, and, best of all for inexperienced painters, you can scrape the paint off and start again.

In times gone by, artists had to employ assistants to grind the pigments laboriously to make up the paint, but today we have no such chores to perform. The paint comes to us in convenient tubes, so that outdoor work presents no problem. The colours are all manufactured to the highest standards possible and there is a wider choice than ever before. There are ready-made canvases and painting boards, as well as brushes to suit all styles and ways of working. Furthermore, new mediums to use with oil paints have made it possible to revive some of the old techniques, such as glazing, which had been largely abandoned by the late 19th century. The oil painter has never been in such a fortunate position.

MADGE BRIGHT
VICTORIAN ROSES IN GLASS
(Above) *Once more, oil paint is the medium used for this lovely painting, which provides a perfect example of the skilful exploitation of a limited colour scheme consisting almost entirely of pinks and dark greens. In spite of its apparent simplicity the painting is meticulously planned and composed, with the mass of the flowerheads creating a strong, irregular shape across the picture, and the stalks arranged to introduce a contrasting linear pattern.*

PAUL BARTLETT

ROOM 15, KATHMORE HOUSE, FALMOUTH
(Left) *Light is the primary theme of this picture, painted in oil on canvas. The colour scheme is similar to that of Karen Raney's painting (below), but here the artist has used a very different technique. The brushstrokes are almost invisible and every detail and texture is described in minute detail.*

KAREN RANEY

CLAIRMONT ROAD
(Above) *Room interiors can make exciting painting subjects, providing opportunities for exploring the effects of light. In this painting, also in oil on canvas, the shadows thrown on the curtain by the window bars have created an intriguing pattern of light on dark, which the artist has made her central theme. She has chosen a tall-format canvas in order to stress the vertical thrust of the composition.*

STEWART GEDDES

ROSE-COLOURED HOUSE, PROVENCE
(Left) *In certain lights, brick and stonework can appear surprisingly rich in colour; the building here, which might have looked dull under a grey sky, has provided the artist with the inspiration for an essay in colour. Colours always appear more vivid by contrast, and he has introduced neutral colours to enhance the warm, glowing hues. The painting is done in oil on board.*

73

OLIVER BEVAN
SHARP CORNER

(Right) *Bevan paints both landscapes and urban scenes, using colour in a way that is not strictly naturalistic but which invokes a powerful atmosphere. In this oil painting, strong contrasts of tone and colour produce a highly dramatic effect, with a slight sense of menace reinforced by the two dark figures and the gravestone shapes in the foreground.*

ANNE VANCATOVA
BLUE INTERIOR

(Left) *Painted in oil on canvas, this evocative and intriguing painting of an interior is a celebration of colour. An intense sky blue is used to cover most of the canvas, and form is picked out with a minimum of dark, linear marks which convey the composition's perspective and touches of yellow-green, red and white which hint at details of the scene such as the evening light outside the windows.*

O
I
L

&

A
C
R
Y
L
I
C

74

TIMOTHY EASTON
RESTORATION
*(Right) The degree of
control in this oil
painting is breathtaking,
with every detail and
texture minutely
described – notice
especially the peeling
paint on the open doors
and the leather jacket
worn by the figure in the
doorway. When figures
are included in a
painting they generally
become the centre of
interest, but here the
power of the geometric
pattern of brilliant blue,
near-black and golden
brown is such that the
figures play a minor
role; the painting can
almost be read as an
abstract composition
in colour.*

**ROSALIND
CUTHBERT**
GIANT
CHRYSANTHEMUM
*(Opposite) One of the
beauties of acrylic is
that, because it is not
oil-based, it can be used
in conjunction with
other water-based paints
as well as with various
drawing media.
Working on paper, the
artist has used acrylic
with gouache paint,
exploiting the contrast
of thick and thin paint
and adding touches of
texture and detail to the
flowerhead and vase by
using the effective
sgraffito technique.*

ACRYLICS

A by-product of the new plastics industry, acrylics were invented in the 1950s. Perhaps because they are such newcomers to the art scene, a certain amount of prejudice against them still exists in some quarters, which is a pity, as they are as versatile as oil paints and have some unique qualities of their own.

One of these – vital from the amateur standpoint – is that they dry very quickly, so that you can overpaint as much as you like. You can, of course, overpaint with oils but, because they are slow-drying, there is always a risk of churning up the colours and creating a muddy mess. Acrylics, once dry, are immovable, so that each new layer completely covers the one below without picking up any colour from it. Another advantage is that you can paint on more or less anything, from paper and board to canvas, and the surface needs no advance preparation, or "priming".

Acrylic paints can be used as "imitation" oils because they behave in much the same

way, but there are differences between the two, both in handling and in make-up. All paints are made from fine-ground pigment particles suspended in liquid and bound with a glue of some kind. In the case of acrylics the liquid is water and the binder is a form of plastic – a polymer resin to be precise. Acrylics are thus water-based, not oil-based and, if they need to be thinned, you use water not oil. Likewise, brushes used with acrylics come clean in water, not white spirit.

The disadvantages of acrylics are that changes to the picture can only be made by overpainting, and the paint dries so fast that it cannot be moved around on the surface to any degree like oil paints can. Also, brushes must always be left in a container of water or washed regularly, otherwise they will be ruined. However, the virtues of acrylics far outweigh these minor vices, and those new to painting could find them the perfect medium with which to begin.

PAINTS, BRUSHES & MEDIUMS

O
I
L

&

A
C
R
Y
L
I
C

Both oils and acrylics come in tubes, though some manufacturers of acrylics also produce them in pots, of about the same size as those used for poster paints. Tubes are the usual choice, but pots have the advantage of minimizing wastage. When

well as for any flat, smooth areas of paint. Sables are the best, but they are expensive (and very easy to ruin), so start with one of the many synthetic substitutes, or a sable and synthetic mixture. There is an excellent range of white nylon brushes specially

NYLON BRUSHES FOR

OIL AND ACRYLIC

acrylic paints are squeezed onto the palette at the beginning of a working session, some paint is usually left at the end which is wasted, having become hard and unworkable. With pots, you can dip in as needed and replace the lid immediately. However, the paint is thinner than that in tubes and is thus less effective for thick, oil-painterly effects.

formulated for acrylic painting, and these can also be used for oils.

MEDIUMS
Both oils and acrylics can be used straight from the tube, but often some medium is used to thin the paint or change its quality. Acrylics are water-based and are thus

BRUSHES
Long-handled bristle brushes are traditionally used for oil painting and are equally satisfactory for acrylic. They are made in three basic shapes: flats, rounds and filberts, all of which make a different kind of brushstroke. Only experience will tell you which ones you prefer, so as with paint colours it is wise to begin with a small range – perhaps two of each type.

Most artists' kits include one or two soft brushes, which are used for small details as

A SELECTION OF MEDIUMS FOR OIL AND ACRYLIC

thinned with more water, while oil paints are diluted with turpentine, a mixture of turpentine and linseed oil, or with linseed oil alone.

Various special mediums are made for particular methods of painting. For both

initially, but you may want to try them later on, so we will be looking at their uses in the section dealing with techniques.

However, if you intend to try acrylics, there is one special medium you may find useful from the start. This is a retarder,

POT ACRYLIC

BRISTLE BRUSHES FOR

OIL AND ACRYLIC

TUBE ACRYLICS

oil and acrylic, for example, there are glazing mediums which make the paint more transparent and thin it without causing it to become runny. For those who like to paint very thickly, impasto mediums bulk the paint out. You won't need any of these

which slows the drying time of the paint, allowing you to manipulate it more easily. It is only used for thick paint, as water affects its performance, but it is a great help for acrylic used in the "oil mode".

PALETTES & PAINTING SURFACES

O
I
L

&

A
C
R
Y
L
I
C

The palettes normally used for oil are made of wood and are either kidney-shaped or rectangular (to fit into the lid of a paintbox). Both have a hole for the thumb so that you can hold them comfortably when you work in the traditional standing position. But you do not have to work standing up, nor do you have to hold the palette. Many artists prefer an improvised palette such as a piece of thick glass or hardboard, which they place on a surface beside them, such as a low table or stool.

Glass is a popular choice for acrylic. Wooden oil-painting palettes are not suitable because the paint cannot be removed easily when dry; you need a non-absorbent surface. The palettes sold especially for acrylic are white plastic. Some people find these satisfactory, but others dislike them, as the glaring white surface makes it difficult to judge the colours when mixing them.

There is one other special palette made for acrylic work, which is particularly useful if you are painting out of doors. This "Stay-Wet" palette is a shallow plastic tray in which there is a top layer of non-absorbent paper and a lower layer of blotting paper. Water is poured into the tray below the blotting paper, the paints are laid out on the top layer, and enough water seeps through from the blotting paper to keep them moist. There is also a transparent plastic lid that fits over the tray, keeping the paint fresh more or less indefinitely.

WORKING SURFACES

The best-known surface for oil painting (also used for acrylic) is stretched canvas – that is, some form of cotton or linen material supported by a wooden frame. Canvases are not cheap, but you can stretch your own quite easily. The larger art shops sell canvas

KIDNEY-SHAPED
WOODEN PALETTE

RECTANGULAR
WOODEN PALETTE

by the metre, and stretchers can be bought in pairs. Another method is to stick the material (which does not have to be canvas; you can use old sheets) onto a stiff board such as hardboard (Masonite). You can do this with animal skin glue (size) or with PVA medium diluted with water.

A primer, or ground, is a layer of paint on top of the canvas or board which, in the case of oil paint, prevents the oil from seeping into the material and damaging it. Most canvases and painting boards now made are intended for both oil and acrylic.

There is a variety of different boards sold for oil and acrylic painting, the best of which are canvas-textured. They form an inexpensive alternative to canvases. You can also paint on hardboard (Masonite) or tough cardboard, but for oil painting you need a primer. The best all-purpose one is acrylic gesso.

You can paint on paper too. For acrylic applied fairly thinly, ordinary cartridge (drawing) paper is fine, but for oil, or acrylic built up thickly, use something more solid, such as heavy watercolour paper.

1 CANVAS BOARD

PAINTING KNIVES

Stretching unprimed canvas

1 When you have assembled the stretchers, use a piece of string to check both diagonal measurements, taking it across one way and then the other. If the second measurement differs from the first, the rectangle is out of alignment.

2 Place the stretcher on the canvas, make pencil marks all the way round at least 5 cm (2 in) from the stretcher, and cut out the canvas.

3 Hammer a tack into the centre of the first long side, and then another one on the opposite side; continue from the centre outwards. You can use a staple gun, but tacks are easier to remove if re-using the stretchers.

4 There are various ways of dealing with corners, but this is one of the simplest. Fold in the corner of the canvas neatly and then hammer in a tack to hold it in place.

5 Fold in the remaining flaps of canvas and tack again. Unprimed canvas should not be stretched too tightly because the priming will shrink it. To stretch ready-primed canvas, you need canvas pliers.

2 STRETCHED AND PRIMED CANVAS   3 CANVAS STRETCHERS   4 RAW CANVAS (UNPRIMED)

PRIMARY & SECONDARY COLOURS

Most non-painters know something about colour, for example many people can name the colours of the spectrum (which are those you see in a rainbow). There are seven of these: violet, indigo, blue, green, yellow, orange and red; they are produced by the dispersal of white light through a prism – different colours have different wave-lengths. But while this kind of knowledge may have its uses in photography or colour printing, it cannot be applied usefully when it comes to painting. The colours of light are absolute, there is just one red, yellow, blue and so on, but artist's pigments are not.

MIXING SECONDARIES

The spectrum colours have given rise to the well-known belief that it is possible to mix

any colour under the sun from the three primary colours alone: red, yellow and blue. The colour pictures in this book are indeed produced from just these three colours (plus black), but paints simply do not work in this way. In colour printing a series of tiny dots of pure colour mixes in the eye (optical mixing), but paints have to be physically combined. More important still, pigments are not pure; there are different versions of each primary colour, so which red, blue and yellow would you choose for mixing up another colour?

The first step to successful colour mixing is to recognize the differences between the primary colours; only then can you discover how to mix the best secondary colours – mixtures of two primaries. If you look at the reds, yellows and blues on the starter

Mixing secondary colours

(Opposite) The top row shows mixtures of "like" primaries – those with a bias towards each other – and the bottom row shows the more muted colours produced by mixing unlike pairs of primaries. In each case the primary colours are shown on the right and left, and the mixtures in the three central divisions. The mixtures nearest to the primary colours have a higher proportion of this colour, while for the central division the colours have been mixed in equal proportions.

A STARTER PALETTE

As a general rule it is wise to begin with as few colours as possible and build up gradually. As you become more experienced you will discover which colours you find difficult or impossible to mix, and you can add to your range accordingly. It is virtually impossible, for example, to achieve good purples and mauves by mixing colours, so artists who specialize in flower painting usually have one or two purples as well as some special reds. The colours shown here will be quite adequate to begin with. They are available in both oils and acrylics, although some acrylic ranges use different names for the colours. For example, some makes of acrylic do not include viridian, but there is a similar colour called phthalocyanine green.

CADMIUM RED	ALIZARIN CRIMSON	CADMIUM YELLOW	LEMON YELLOW
ULTRAMARINE	PRUSSIAN BLUE	CERULEAN BLUE	YELLOW OCHRE
VIRIDIAN	RAW UMBER	IVORY BLACK	TITANIUM WHITE

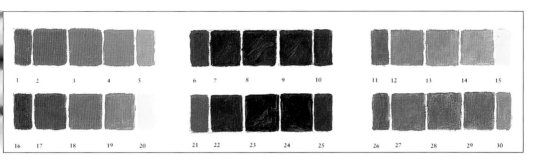

1 CADMIUM RED 2, 3 AND 4 MIXTURES 5 CADMIUM YELLOW 6 ALIZARIN CRIMSON 7, 8 AND 9 MIXTURES 10 ULTRAMARINE 11 CERULEAN 12, 13 AND 14 MIXTURES 15 LEMON YELLOW 16 ALIZARIN CRIMSON 17, 18 AND 19 MIXTURES 20 LEMON YELLOW 21 CADMIUM RED 22, 23 AND 24 MIXTURES 25 ULTRAMARINE 26 CERULEAN 27, 28 AND 29 MIXTURES 30 CADMIUM YELLOW

1 ORANGE (CADMIUM RED AND YELLOW) 2 PLUS BLACK 3 ORANGE 4 PLUS WHITE 5 PURPLE (ALIZARIN CRIMSON AND ULTRAMARINE) 6 PLUS BLACK 7 PURPLE 8 PLUS WHITE 9 GREEN (CERULEAN AND LEMON YELLOW) 10 PLUS BLACK 11 GREEN 12 PLUS WHITE 13 MUTED ORANGE 14 PLUS BLACK 15 MUTED ORANGE 16 PLUS WHITE 17 PURPLE BROWN 18 PLUS BLACK 19 PURPLE BROWN 20 PLUS WHITE 21 GREEN 22 PLUS BLACK 23 GREEN 24 PLUS WHITE

Adding black and white *(Above)* These "swatches" give an idea of the large range of colours which can be made by adding black or white to mixtures. The 50:50 mixtures of primary colours shown in the chart above have been taken as the basis, with first black and then white added.

palette, you will see that they have different biases. One red leans towards purple or blue, and the other is more orange; lemon yellow is greener than cadmium yellow; ultramarine is slightly redder than cerulean or Prussian blue. The most vivid secondary colours are made by mixing primaries which are biased towards each other. You cannot make a good, bright orange, for example, with lemon yellow and alizarin crimson, or a good purple with cadmium red and ultramarine.

Making charts like the ones shown here, using the six basic primary colours, first on their own and then with the addition of black and white, will teach you a great deal about colour. As well as finding out how to make bright secondary colours, you may discover some useful mixtures for more muted effects. If so, try to remember them, as many paintings are spoilt by muddy, characterless neutrals. For example, an interesting grey is often made from a mixture of colours, not black and white.

USING A RESTRICTED PALETTE

Painting with a limited range of colours is an exercise often set in art schools. In this case the idea is to use only the six basic primary colours: cadmium red, alizarin crimson, cadmium and lemon yellow, ultramarine and Prussian blue; plus white. You are not allowed black because, although a useful colour, it is also a seductive one; you may feel tempted to take the easy way out by adding it whenever you want to darken a colour, and this can lead to muddy, dull mixtures. White is permitted because there is no other way to lighten colours when you are using opaque paints, but you may discover that white is not always the answer. Adding white to red, for instance, turns it pink, so it is sometimes better to add yellow instead.

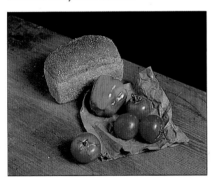

Choose a simple still-life group like the one shown here, but make sure you have plenty of colour contrast and some good dark areas to test your ability to make dark colours without black. You can use either oil or acrylic – the exercise is about mixing colours rather than handling paints.

COLOURS USED (OIL PAINTS) *titanium white, Prussian blue, alizarin crimson, ultramarine, cadmium red, lemon yellow, cadmium yellow*

Still life in six hues

1 *The colour used here, which looks very similar to yellow ochre, has been mixed from white, lemon yellow and a little cadmium red.*

2 *For the tomatoes, the artist uses a mixture of both reds, with an added touch of lemon yellow for the lighter areas. He leaves the white of the board to show through for the highlights.*

3 *The basic green for the pepper is ultramarine and cadmium yellow, two colours which can be mixed in varying proportions to produce a good range of greens.*

6 (Above) *The artist has had no difficulty in mixing all the colours in the group from these six, and could even have reduced the number to five, by excluding the Prussian blue.*

4 *The brown for the loaf of bread is similar to the colour used in Step 1, but slightly darkened with small additions of alizarin crimson and ultramarine.*

5 (Right) *Prussian blue, a very strong, dark colour which must be used sparingly, is now mixed with both reds and yellows for the background. A similar mixture, but with more Prussian blue, was used for the leaves on the tomatoes.*

COLOUR RELATIONSHIPS

Establishing how to mix colours similar to the ones you observe is a vital step in the business of learning to paint, but you also need to understand something about how colours relate to each other. No colour exists in isolation – it is defined by juxtaposition and contrast with other colours. An orange or lemon placed on a neutral-coloured or dark cloth shines out because of the strong contrast, but the same fruit on an orange or yellow cloth forms no contrast, and thus creates little impact.

The fruit on a dark cloth would make use of contrasts of tone, which means the lightness or darkness of a colour. Tonal contrasts are important in painting, but there are other kinds of contrast too. Bright colours can contrast with neutral ones, and so-called "warm" colours with "cool" ones.

TEMPERATURE

Artists often describe colours in terms of "temperature", a visual and partially subjective quality that cannot be measured. Blues, blue-greens and blue-greys are cool, while reds, yellows and colours with red and yellow in them are warm.

Warm–cool contrasts are a way of creating the impression of space and recession in a painting. This is because the warm colours tend to advance to the front of the picture and the cool ones to recede further into the background.

But everything in colour is relative; even a colour ordinarily described as cool may lose its recessive habit if there is an insufficient contrast of warm colours. To complicate matters further, there are warm and cool versions of each colour. Ultramarine, which has a red bias, is warmer than cerulean or Prussian blue, and cadmium yellow is warmer than the slightly acid lemon yellow, which leans towards green.

NEUTRALS

These colours, the greys, browns, beiges and all the indeterminate ones in between, are often dismissed as unimportant. But, in fact, they have a vital role to play: they act as a foil for the bright colours and provide a framework for them.

The trouble with neutrals is that, because they are often difficult to analyse, it is hard to know which colours to start mixing. Furthermore, they are only neutral by virtue of contrast; for example, a greenish grey that takes a definite back seat when juxtaposed with red can look quite vivid when set against the ultimate neutral – a mixture of black and white.

Apart from the latter, which has no colour at all and should seldom, if ever, be used in painting, all neutral colours have their own colour biases. Greys are yellowish, brownish, slightly blue or tending towards mauve. This means that they must fit in with the colour bias of your painting. A useful device is to scrape your palette with a palette knife halfway through a working session and use this subtle colour mixture for neutrals. This ensures that the neutrals, being a mixture of all the colours used, will work in the context of the painting. You can do this only in oil, unfortunately, as acrylic dries too quickly on the palette.

Another good way of neutralizing a colour is to use its complementary. Complementary colours are those that are opposite each other on a colour wheel: red and green, violet and yellow, orange and blue. When these pairs of vivid opposite colours are mixed together they cancel each other out, making subtle neutrals that vary according to the proportions of the colours used. Successful neutrals always give a painting much more impact.

Warm and cool colours
As can be seen here, the warm colours, the reds, oranges and yellows, push forward in front of the cooler greens and blues. However, the orange does not advance as much on warmer blue.

Relative values
The colours in the centres of the first two squares are cool, but do not recede because the surrounding colours are cooler still. In the second pair, all the colours are warm, but the alizarin crimson and lemon yellow are cooler than the orange.

Neutrals
All the colours shown in the swatches are neutral, made from black and white with small additions of other colours. Seen in isolation they do not seem to be any particular colour, though some have biases towards red, green or blue. However, the squares at the bottom show how differently they appear depending on their surroundings. In the first and third squares a neutral colour is shown against a vivid background, while in the second and fourth the background is a neutral grey made from black and white.

ORANGE ON ULTRAMARINE   CADMIUM RED ON BLUE-GREEN   ORANGE ON CERULEAN BLUE   LEMON YELLOW ON GREEN

ULTRAMARINE ON PRUSSIAN BLUE   YELLOW-GREEN ON BLUE-GREEN   ORANGE ON ALIZARIN   CADMIUM YELLOW ON LEMON YELLOW

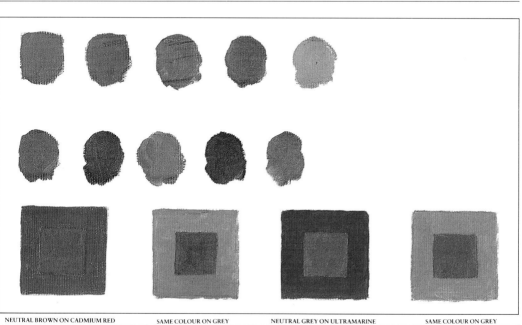

NEUTRAL BROWN ON CADMIUM RED   SAME COLOUR ON GREY   NEUTRAL GREY ON ULTRAMARINE   SAME COLOUR ON GREY

PAINTING WHITE

There is no better way of learning how to analyse and mix neutral colours than by painting one or two bright-coloured objects on a white background. You will also discover how radically light affects colour. Dark colours absorb the light but white is reflective, so when you look at a white object you see a marvellous range of subtle colours and probably very little pure white, or even none at all. The colours vary according to the kind of light you are working under, and on the objects, which can throw colour into the nearby shadows. Unfortunately, as the light changes so do the colours – a particular problem if your group is set up near a window. But it is a challenging task and well worth trying.

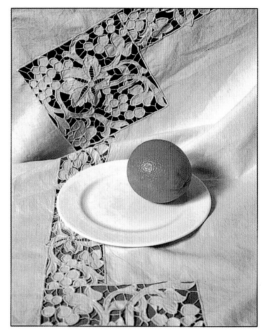

COLOURS USED *black, ultramarine, cerulean blue, Indian red, cadmium red, Venetian red, burnt umber, yellow ochre, cadmium yellow, lemon yellow, titanium white*

1 *As the orange is the brightest colour in the group, it has been blocked in first. This provides a key, enabling the artist to assess the grey-greens and blue-greens for the plate and background.*

2 *He moves on to the area of strongest tonal contrast, drawing in the pattern of the cloth with a fine sable brush.*

3 *As he works, he carefully assesses one colour against another. The greys of the cloth are far from being colourless, although they are neutral in comparison with the orange.*

4 The middle tones of the cloth have been established before the lightest areas, where the folds of the cloth catch the light. Here the artist has used pure white, but has painted lightly so that the brushstroke is broken up by the texture of the canvas, and a little of the underlying colour shows through.

6 The artist has worked on fine canvas stretched over board and lightly tinted with a wash of watercolour. He finds that a coloured ground makes it easier to judge the tones of his mixtures, and in a subject such as this, with a predominance of light tones, it is particularly helpful.

5 The orange and the plate have been solidly built up and final touches are now given to the background. The tonal contrasts here must not be too strong, so the white is mixed with a little yellow and red to darken and warm it.

WORKING ALLA PRIMA

n

O
I
L

&

A
C
R
Y
L
I
C

Students often want to know how to build up an oil painting – where should they start and what are the stages? These are not easy questions to answer, as there are so many different ways of doing things. Oil-painting techniques have changed through the centuries; besides which, individual artists have their own methods.

A REVOLUTION IN TECHNIQUE
The most important change in technique was brought about by the French Impressionists in the 19th century, who overturned many earlier ideas, not only about methods but also about the whole nature of art. Previously, oil paintings had been built up in layers, beginning with a monochrome underpainting on a mid-toned ground. This established the composition, the modelling of forms and the whole tonal structure of the work. The colour was added only as a final stage. These paintings were done in the studio, with location work restricted to small studies.

The Impressionists worked out of doors direct from their subject, abandoning the complex layering method entirely and always completing a painting in one session. This method, known as working "alla prima", which means "at first", rapidly became the norm, particularly for outdoor work, where speed is vital. However, many of the older methods are now being revived in modified forms and some artists prefer to work over an underpainting, a method which is discussed on the following pages.

WET INTO WET
The term "alla prima" does not describe one specific technique because there are different ways of starting and completing a painting in one go. There is, however, one feature that characterizes alla prima paintings: that of blending colours wet into wet. When paint is allowed to dry before further layers are added, each new brushstroke is crisp and well-defined, but laying one colour over and into still-wet

Working wet into wet

1 *Working in oil on canvas board, the artist begins with the paint used thinly, diluted with turpentine alone. White spirit can also be used, but turpentine, being slightly oily, gives a more lustrous surface.*

2 *Having blocked in the flowers, still with fairly thin paint, she blends dark green into the still-wet paint beneath. She uses a sable rather than a bristle brush, as this makes a softer impression.*

3 *A soft, blurred highlight is now created by wiping into the paint with a rag. The first layer of blue-green, which is now dry, remains in place.*

6 (Left) *In any oil painting, but particularly for wet-into-wet methods, it is best to begin with thin paint and build up gradually to thicker applications, otherwise the paint becomes unmanageable. Here the thickest colour has been used for the red flowers.*

4 (Right) *The paint is now used more thickly, slightly diluted with a mixture of linseed oil and turpentine, and the brushstrokes are gently blended into one another.*

5 (Right) *White is applied lightly over the wet red paint so that the two colours mix together on the surface, to produce a gentle pink highlight.*

paint creates a gentler, less decisive effect, as each new colour is modified by the one below. The Impressionists painted wet into wet extensively – the soft, slightly blurred effects you see in Monet's beautiful paintings of water and foliage were achieved in this way.

The method is not quite as easy as it sounds; you need a light touch and it's best to avoid too much overworking. Too many colours laid one over another can result in a churned-up mess of paint, with no colour or definition. If this happens, scrape the area back with a palette knife and start again. It is only possible to work wet into wet in acrylic if you use a made-for-the-purpose retarding medium to keep the paint moist and workable.

UNDERPAINTING

Most artists make a drawing on their working surface before they begin to paint; this can be a brush drawing or one made with pencil or charcoal. Some take this framework for the painting one step further, making a full-scale underpainting in monochrome. This allows them to plan the composition and the tonal structure of the picture before putting on the colour.

A monochrome underpainting need not be in shades of grey – monochrome simply means one colour. Another function of the underpainting is to provide contrasts of colour; sometimes areas of underpainting are left to show through in the finished work, or the paint is applied thinly enough to be modified by the colour of the underpainting – a method often used in conjunction with glazing techniques in either oil or acrylic. The Renaissance painters liked to use a green underpainting, building up warm skin tones with thin layers of colour. In the same way a warm red or yellow underpainting could be tried for a subject in which greens and blues predominate.

More than one colour can be used – underpainting simply means a layer of paint below the top layer. Some artists begin their paintings by covering the whole canvas with "washes" of very thin paint, heavily diluted with turpentine; they allow this to dry and then build up gradually to thicker paint. Because oil paints can be used over acrylic (but not vice versa), acrylic is sometimes used for the earlier stages of paintings built up in this way, although oil paint thinned with turpentine also dries quite quickly.

Underpainting in acrylic

1 The artist begins with thin washes of diluted grey-green acrylic, gradually building up the basic forms of the face and head. She is working on canvas board.

2 The underpainting is now complete, providing a tonal basis on which the colours can be applied. Although working in acrylic, she uses the traditional method of beginning with thin paint.

3 She now turns to oil paint, still using it thinly for the hair and then slightly more thickly for the warm colour of the forehead.

5 *The oil paint is thicker for the highlights and details of the features, but in places the underpainting is still visible; you can see the original grey-green on the hair and beneath the left eye.*

6 (Below) *The colour chosen for the underpainting depends on the effect you want to achieve. This dull green is a traditional choice for portraits and figure work, as it helps to establish a contrast between shadow areas and warmer highlights.*

4 *The colour used for the forehead has been blended lightly into the underpainting to give a soft gradation of tone. The mauve-blues of the background have been kept thin by diluting the oil paint with turpentine.*

FROM LEAN TO FAT

Nowadays there are few hard-and-fast rules in oil painting but, if you are building up a painting in layers, you must always work from "lean" to "fat", or from thin paint to thick. When diluted (lean) paint is laid over thick, oily (fat) paint, cracking may occur due to the top layer drying before the bottom one, which shrinks slightly as it dries. Apart from these technical considerations, saving the thick paint until last also minimizes the risk of churning it up by subsequent painting over the top.

WORKING ON A TINTED GROUND

Up until the middle of the 19th century it was standard oil-painting practice to work on canvas which had been given an overall tint, called an *imprimatura*. The Impressionists abandoned this practice, as they did so many others, and worked on white canvas, which they found increased the brilliance of the colours (though Monet returned to coloured grounds at various stages in his career).

Today's artists are divided on this issue, but there is no doubt that a coloured ground can be very helpful. White is an artificial colour (there is little or no true white in nature) so beginning with a white surface makes it difficult to judge the strength of the first colours you apply. You may make them too light, because any colour looks dark against white. Colouring the canvas provides an average tone, allowing you to work up to the lightest areas and down to the dark ones.

The choice of colour will influence your painting from the start. The most usual choices are neutrals such as browns, yellow-browns, greys and blue-greys. These are useful base shades on which to apply brighter colours. Some artists like a ground which contrasts with the overall colour scheme, for example warm brown for a painting in which blues will predominate; others prefer one which harmonizes. In either case, small areas of the ground colour are sometimes allowed to show through between brushstrokes, which has the effect of pulling the picture together, or unifying it, by creating a series of colour links. In this way a coloured ground can act very much like an underpainting.

Laying a ground is very easy and you can use either acrylic, watercolour or oil paint thinned with white spirit – obviously one of the first two if you are working in acrylic. Spread the paint over the surface either with a large brush or with a rag. It doesn't matter if you create an uneven, streaky effect; a completely flat colour tends to look mechanical and unappealing.

Acrylic on a blue ground

1 *The ground colour chosen for oil paintings is most frequently an unobtrusive brown or grey, but acrylic encourages a bolder approach; a deep blue is used here. The artist, working on watercolour paper, applies the ground with a large nylon brush for quick coverage of the surface.*

2 *She begins with the light area of sky, painting boldly with another large, square-ended nylon brush. The paint is used quite thickly, mixed with just enough water to make it malleable. She has not made a preliminary drawing because acrylic can easily be corrected by overpainting.*

3 *Dark green is now painted over the blue, this time using a smaller bristle brush to make dabbing brushstrokes which do not completely cover the blue ground colour. The paint is also used quite thinly to modify the blue without obscuring it.*

6 *(Above) The dark reflections beneath were slightly blurred by glazing over them with well-watered paint, applied with a large, soft brush.*

4 *To create the blurred effect of the water, black paint is lightly scrubbed over the underlying colours, which are now dry. Again, care is taken not to cover all of the blue underpainting.*

5 *In the final stages, a definite centre of interest is created by introducing a vivid yellow-green into the small tree.*

BRUSHWORK

As the natural consistency of both oil and acrylic paints is thick and creamy, they hold the marks of the brush very well and, for any paintings except those built up in smooth layers or glazes, brushwork is an integral part of the painting. The idea of exploiting the physical presence of the paint began with artists such as Titian in the 16th century and Rembrandt in the 17th; it was developed further by the Impressionists and further still by Cézanne and Van Gogh – the two artists one automatically associates with brushwork.

Many promising paintings are spoiled by inattention to brushwork. This is understandable when there are so many other things to consider, such as working out how to mix the colours, getting the drawing right, and the general business of depicting your subject. But brushwork needs as much consideration as any other aspect of the painting; in fact, it can help you in the task of description. If you are painting a tree trunk, for example, or you want to suggest the sweep of a hill or field, it is easier to use a large brush and let it do the work by following the forms and directions than it is to build up the shape with a series of small, fussy strokes.

One thing you need to guard against is inconsistency of brushwork. Your brushstrokes do not all have to go in the same direction or be the same size (though they can be), but you must use the same approach throughout. If the sky in a landscape is painted flatly, and bold, sweeping brushstrokes are used to depict trees and hills, the picture looks disjointed. Skies can be problematic because they do appear flat, but here you must use artistic licence. Paintings by Cézanne clearly reveal individual brushmarks in the sky area as well as a variety of different colours.

Exploiting the brushmarks

1 *Working in oil on oil-sketching paper, the artist uses her bristle brush as a drawing implement, making sweeping strokes to describe the shapes of the hills.*

2 *It is not necessary to use thick paint to exploit brushmarks, and here it is quite thin (it has been diluted with turpentine). This gives the brushstrokes an uneven striated quality, with the white paper showing through in some areas.*

Brushes are made in different shapes as well as different sizes, and it is worth experimenting with them to discover the kinds of mark they can make. Cézanne used mainly large flat brushes, which give a brick-like stroke, whereas Monet favoured pointed ones, applying the paint in smaller dabs. Try out all your brushes, holding them in different ways and varying the pressure to make different kinds of strokes. This kind of doodling will help you to discover your own painting style.

3 (Above) *The paint is used more thickly here, but the brushwork is similar to that depicting the land area. The artist uses long, sweeping strokes, letting the brushmarks follow the direction of the hills.*

4 *The paint was used thinly in the early stages and the first applications are now dry; consequently, brushstrokes of thicker paint can be laid without disturbing those below.*

5 *The brush is used in a different direction, with more upward strokes, again of thicker paint, suggesting the stone wall in the middle distance without describing it literally.*

6 (Below) *The brushwork is consistent throughout the painting, and not only describes the forms of the landscape but also imparts movement and energy to the picture.*

IMPASTO

Impasto means thicker-than-usual paint. For some artists, one of the main attractions of oil and acrylic is that they can be built up thickly to create a range of exciting surface textures.

Impasto techniques are far from new. Both Rembrandt and the great 19th-century landscape painter, J.M.W. Turner, used thick, solid paint in some areas of their paintings, contrasting this with thinner applications elsewhere. In some of Rembrandt's portraits, too, the faces, particularly the highlight areas, are so solidly built up that they resemble a relief sculpture. Van Gogh was the first artist to use uniformly thick paint, applied in swirling or jagged brushstrokes; since then many artists have exploited the expressive and dynamic qualities of thick paint, sometimes squeezing it on straight from the tube and then modelling it with a brush, or applying it with a knife or even fingers.

Impasto of this nature requires a great deal of paint, so it is a good idea to bulk it out with one of the special media sold for impasto work in both oil and acrylic. This is particularly necessary for acrylic, as it is slightly runnier than oil. The media are effective, enabling you to produce two or three times the amount of paint without changing the colour. The only other way to bulk up paint is to add white.

Impasto used selectively, for specific areas of the painting, is usually reserved for finishing touches, highlights or any small areas of vivid colour in the foreground. There is a good reason for this: thick paint, having a more powerful physical presence than thin paint, tends to advance to the front of the picture.

Using thickened paint

1 *This photograph shows the oil paint being mixed with special impasto medium (the brownish substance on the left). Similar mediums are available for working in acrylic.*

2 *Sometimes impasto is reserved for certain areas of a painting, usually added in the final stages, but here thick paint is used throughout. At this stage, each area of colour is kept separate to avoid mixing and muddying.*

3 *In this sky area, the brush is taken in different directions, creating ridges and swirls of paint which reflect the light in varying degrees.*

6 (Left) *Finally, with deft touches made with the tip of the brush, darker colours were laid over and into the light yellow-browns on the tree trunks. Paint applied as thickly as this takes several days to dry out thoroughly.*

5 (Right) *To produce a soft blend of colours, dark green is worked into a lighter one, wet into wet. The top and edges of the dark green foliage have also been softened by painting over the light grey of the sky.*

4 *Again, the artist takes care to keep each new colour separate. If the thick dark green paint were allowed to mix with the lighter colour, both would become muddied.*

KNIFE PAINTING

A brush is the most obvious implement for applying paint, and the most commonly used, but paint can also be put on with a knife made for the purpose. Knife painting is an exciting and expressive technique, and it creates effects quite different from any which can be achieved with a brush. The knife squeezes and flattens the paint on the surface, producing a smooth plane with ridges at the edges.

These small ridges and lines of thicker paint catch the light and, when a whole painting is built up with knife marks, they create an energetic and lively effect. Like brushstrokes, the marks can be varied according to their direction, their size, the amount of pressure you apply and the thickness of the paint. But take care not to overwork; too many knife strokes laid over one another will sacrifice the crispness which characterizes the method, creating a muddled impression.

Like any other impasto technique, knife painting can be used selectively to emphasize certain areas of the painting. For a floral subject, you might use a flick of the knife to suggest a highlight on the vase or a leaf catching the light, while in landscape you could enliven a dull foreground with some fine strokes made with the side of the knife, depicting long stems of grass, or make small dabs with the point of a knife to create colourful flowerheads.

Painting knives are surprisingly delicate and sensitive instruments. They are not to be confused with the ordinary straight-bladed palette knife used for general cleaning up. These knives are specially made for the job; they have cranked handles and highly flexible forged-steel blades, and are produced in a wide variety of different shapes and sizes.

Knife-painted flowers

1 *To provide a background for the colours of the flowers and leaves, the artist has begun with thin "washes" of oil paint, which she has allowed to dry before putting on the first knife strokes.*

2 *Using the point of the knife, she now flicks on thick, dark colour for the stems. The flowers are still essentially a thin veil of colour, achieved by laying on paint and then scraping it back with the side of the knife.*

3 *A light blue-green is laid over the darker colour with the flat of the knife. Notice how this flattens and pushes the paint so that it is thinner in the centre of the stroke, only lightly covering the canvas.*

4 (Right) *The flowers are built up with a combination of strokes using the point and side of the knife. This small triangular knife is ideal for chrysanthemums and similar flowers, as each petal can be quickly created with a single sharp flick.*

5 (Above) *Grey-green background colour is now "cut in" around the stems and leaves with the flat of the knife. If the flowers and leaves had been painted over thick, wet background paint, the colours would have mixed together and lost their brightness.*

6 (Left) *The flowers and leaves are convincingly depicted, and the liveliness of the picture is increased by the contrast between thick and thin paint. The knife work stands out from the surface, while in some areas of the background the canvas is only lightly stained with colour.*

GLAZING

O
I
L
&
A
C
R
Y
L
I
C

Glazing is one of the traditional techniques that is regaining popularity – and for good reason, as it can create beautiful effects. The painters of the early Renaissance used oil paints very thinly, building up layers of transparent colour. The brilliant blues and reds you see in the gowns of madonnas and saints were achieved by this method.

Glazing used to be a slow process because each layer had to dry before the next one was applied, so when alla prima painting became the most usual way of working, glazing was largely abandoned. Now, however, the paint manufacturers have brought out special glazing media which cut down the drying time of oil and make the colours more transparent.

In acrylic, glazing takes no time at all because the paints dry so fast, and so the method is particularly popular with acrylic painters. The paint can be thinned with water, or with acrylic medium (matt or gloss). The latter is usually preferable, as paint thinned with water alone dries to a dull, matt finish, while the medium gives it a slight or high gloss – depending on which one you use – which enriches the colours.

Glazes can also be laid over thick paint, as long as it is dry. In acrylic particularly, thick impastos made with a brush or knife are often modified by glazes, which give a touch of delicacy to the heavy surface. This is also a good way to suggest texture, because the colours settle into the crevices.

If you intend to experiment with glazing you may have to consider buying some extra colours. Although both oil and acrylic are technically opaque, some pigments are relatively transparent. As the essence of glazing is the way one layer of colour shows through another, the best results are achieved by sticking to the more transparent colours.

Building up colours

Instead of using full-strength opaque colour from the start, it is possible to build up with a series of glazes. The "swatches" shown here are in acrylic, but similar effects can be achieved in oil, or oil can be glazed over acrylic.

Changing colours

One colour glazed over another produces a third colour by modifying the one below. Here the top colours have been thinned with acrylic medium, which makes them more transparent.

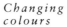

Toning down

If colours appear too bright in one area of a painting they can be neutralized by laying a light glaze of acrylic diluted with water. Water glazes cannot, of course, be used in oil painting, but oil paint can be thinned with glazing medium.

Glazing over monochrome

In either oil or acrylic, a picture can be started in monochrome – black and white or shades of one colour – and glazes subsequently laid on top.

BROKEN COLOUR

When you drag oil or acrylic paint lightly over a textured canvas or a layer of dry paint, it adheres only to the peaks, thus breaking up the brushstroke and allowing some of the earlier colour to remain visible. This method, called dry brush, is particularly suitable for creating veils of colour or for suggesting texture. It is frequently employed in landscape, for example, for light on water, distant trees or the texture of grass, while in portraiture it is useful for hair and textured clothing. The trick is to apply the minimum of paint to the brush and to use a fairly thick, dry mixture.

A similar method, scumbling, gives you less control and is more suitable for large areas than for fine detail. It involves scrubbing thick, dry paint over another colour, either with a rag, a stiff bristle brush or even your fingers. You can scumble dark colours over light, but light over dark usually achieves the best results. You might use the method for skies in a landscape (scumbling light blue over deep blue to produce a shimmering effect), or for richly coloured fabric in a portrait or still life.

The effects of these methods are sometimes described as "broken colour" – a term which has an alternative meaning, referring to an area built up with small brushstrokes of separate colours. This technique was more or less invented by the Impressionists, who found that they could make areas of grass or foliage appear brighter by juxtaposing blues, yellows, greens and sometimes purples, which from a distance would be interpreted as green.

Dry brush in acrylic

1 *The artist has begun with an underpainting of rich blue-green for the land, with transparent washes for the sky. She now drags thick paint lightly over.*

2 *For the foreground she uses the same brush but makes shorter, more upright strokes, varying them to suggest both the texture and movement of the grass.*

3 *The field in the centre is the deepest area of colour in the picture; not wanting to cover too much of the underpainting, the artist uses a colour which is only slightly lighter, applying it with horizontal sweeps.*

4 *(Right) As well as being the ideal method for suggesting texture, dry brush also creates a livelier effect than flat areas of colour. It is best to work on a textured surface – this picture has been done on canvas board.*

REMOVING PAINT

The first two methods described here are not suitable for acrylic, as they rely on the slow-drying nature of oil paints.

SCRAPING BACK

When something goes wrong with an oil painting, you can scrape back the offending area or even the whole painting with a palette knife – as long as the paint is still wet – and repaint it. If you have ever done this, you may have noticed that the effect of the scraped painting is rather attractive – a misty ghost image of the original picture.

Scraping back need not be limited to correcting mistakes; it can be a technique in its own right. It has been employed by several well-known artists, most notably the 19th-century American-born artist James Whistler, who often scraped back his portraits at the end of each day's session in order to avoid overworking his paint and, on one occasion, observed that this gave him exactly the effect he wanted for the gauzy dress of his young girl sitter.

Scraping back is a layering technique, similar in some ways to glazing, as each new application of colour, after scraping, reveals something of the colours below. You can use it to build up subtle colour effects, or to create the impression of a misty landscape. If you work on a textured surface such as canvas or canvas board, the knife removes the colour only from the top of the raised grain, leaving a deposit of paint in between the weave.

1 *Working on canvas board – stretched canvas could be damaged by scraping – the artist lays thick paint on the sky and hills and scrapes over it with the side of a palette knife.*

2 *Having begun with a wash of yellow-green which has now dried, she then laid darker, thicker colour which she partially scrapes away. This time she uses a plastic credit card, a useful if unusual painting tool.*

3 *The foreground has been darkened with successive applications of paint, each subsequently scraped back. The artist now uses the card first to apply paint and then to scrape it back in diagonal strokes.*

4 *(Right) The technique is particularly useful for atmospheric effects and subtle blends of colour. Finger smudging has been used in places, and the shapes in the foreground were made by using the plastic card as a painting knife.*

Scratching into paint

1 *Having laid a foundation of relatively thick oil paint on canvas board, a paintbrush handle is used to draw into it, creating ridges and indentations.*

2 *The point of a scalpel removes the paint more cleanly and thoroughly, revealing the surface of the canvas beneath in a series of fine white lines.*

3 *Drawing into wet paint with a pencil is a variation of sgraffito. The pencil makes dark lines as well as similar indentations to those produced by the paintbrush handle.*

4 *(Above) This method is useful for textures and ideal for making the kind of very fine lines which are difficult to achieve with a paintbrush, such as stalks of grass or tiny twigs catching the light.*

SGRAFFITO

This involves scoring or scribbling into the paint while it is still wet – the word comes from the Italian *sgraffiare*, to scratch. Rembrandt used to scribble into thick, wet paint with a brush handle to suggest the hairs of a moustache or the pattern and texture of clothing. Working into thick paint in this way produces an indented furrow, with slight ridges where the paint has been pushed upwards. This can be a useful method for describing textures.

Sgraffito can also be used in a purely decorative way to add a pattern element to your work. If the top application of paint is thin, you can scratch into it with a sharp implement to reveal the white of the canvas, or another dry colour below. For example, the objects in a still life could be outlined with fine white lines or you could create the pattern on a piece of fabric by scratching back to another colour. Although sgraffito is easier in oil, it can be done with acrylic too, as it is possible to scratch into dry paint providing you work on a rigid surface such as a painting board.

TONKING

Invented by Sir Henry Tonks, one-time professor at the Slade School of Art in London, tonking is another correction method which can be utilized as a technique. An oil painting often reaches a stage where it is unworkable because there is such a heavy build-up of paint that any new colours simply mingle with the earlier ones, producing a muddy, churned-up mess. Tonks recommended removing the top layer of paint by laying a sheet of newspaper over the painting and rubbing gently to transfer the paint to the paper. The resulting softened image can be a basis for further work, but often the effect is pleasing in itself; you can leave the tonked painting alone, or perhaps add touches of further definition in certain areas. Tonking is particularly useful for any painting in which you have tried to add too much detail too early on, such as a portrait, where the eyes and mouth tend to attract a concentration of paint.

COMPARATIVE DEMONSTRATION

O
I
L
&
A
C
R
Y
L
I
C

Oil and acrylic paints can be used in many different ways. One of the best ways of learning, at least initially, is to attempt to emulate the methods of artists whose work you admire. In order to provide a stimulus as well as to show something of the possible variations in approach, we have asked three artists to paint the same still life subject. James Horton is working in oil, on fine canvas stretched over board, primed with whiting and rabbit-skin glue and tinted with watercolour, giving a slightly absorbent and lightly coloured surface. Patrick Cullen is also working in oil, but on white canvas board. Rosalind Cuthbert is painting in acrylic on paper, making considerable use of glazing methods.

Oil on primed and tinted canvas

1 *The artist has begun with a brush drawing (in a mixture of Venetian red and raw umber) to establish the shapes and position of the bottles, and now works on the warm colours of the background. It is important to have some of this colour in place before painting the bottles.*

2 *His method is to place small patches of colour all over the picture surface in order to assess the relationships of colour and tone at every stage in the painting.*

3 *Darker tones have now been introduced into the bottles, and he returns to work on the background, using a lighter colour to bring out the dark greens.*

(Right) *Various artists' palettes give an interesting insight into their various working methods. In this case the "brushstrokes" used to mix the colours reflect those in the painting itself.*

4 With the painting at about the halfway stage, the brushwork is still loose, with the surface not yet fully covered. The paint is used at the same consistency throughout, slightly thinned with a mixture of turpentine, linseed oil and Damar varnish.

5 Ellipses are always tricky and, in spite of careful initial drawing, have to be maintained through the course of the painting. Here the edge of the label is defined by cutting in darker paint around the bottom.

6 (Right) In the final stages, details were added, such as the suggestion of printing on the label, the cork of the bottle and the ellipse of the glass. Notice how varied the brushwork is, and the many different colours used in each area of the picture.

Continued ▷

—

1 The artist began with a drawing in soft pencil, erasing from time to time until it was correct. He uses the paint quite thinly, diluting it with a 50:50 mixture of synthetic medium and turpentine.

2 A difference in approach in the early stages is immediately apparent. This artist takes each part of the painting close to completion before beginning on the next; here he works extensively on the bottle.

The artist prefers a large kidney-shaped palette to the small rectangular type which fits into the lid of a paintbox. Once more, the brushwork in the painting is echoed in the palette.

3 The first bottle is now virtually finished, and the second one is painted before the background. The white board shows through the thin paint in places to suggest the transparency of the glass.

4 With the background and the wine glass now painted, finishing touches are given to the bottle. A soft highlight is created by rubbing into the wet paint with a clean rag.

5 When painting transparent objects it is vital to ensure the continuity of the background, so this has been painted first, leaving the highlights and shadows of the glass until last.

6 The biggest difference between this and the previous painting is in the consistency of paint, which here has been wiped off to create highlights rather than added as thicker paint. The brushwork in both paintings is lively and varied, but each artist has a distinctive style.

1 The artist begins with a thin under-painting diluted with water, lightly sketching in the shapes of the bottles. She seldom makes an initial drawing when using opaque paints.

2 Her method is to build up the more subtle colours by glazing in successive layers over a brightly coloured base, so initially she uses blue for the bottles and a rich red for the background.

These Stay-Wet palettes look far from attractive after a day's work, but they are ideal for preventing acrylic paint from drying out.

3 Paint mixed with matt medium is laid over the blue. While still wet the colour looks opaque, but it becomes more transparent as the medium dries.

4 On the left-hand bottle you can see the effect of the glazing method clearly – the paint has now dried and each colour shows through the other. Slightly thicker paint is now used for the background.

5 As in the previous two demonstrations, the glass is left until last. The highlights on the ellipse are painted, again with a fine sable brush, but this time with thicker paint, straight from the tube.

6 This artist has taken a less literal and more personal approach to the group than the other two, inventing a blue background and keying up the colours. She has also deliberately distorted the right-hand bottle to improve the composition.

STILL LIFE

Throughout the history of painting, still life has gone in and out of fashion, mainly according to the whims of buyers. Still-life paintings were particularly sought after in 16th- and 17th-century Holland, while in France and England they were less popular nationally, although there were certain areas where this branch of painting flourished. In the 19th century, when more humble, down-to-earth subject matters began to replace grandiose historical works, still life came into its own; since that time many artists have painted still life in addition to other subjects, and some have made it their speciality.

There is no better way of practising your skills and working out ideas about colour and composition than by choosing and arranging your own subject. When you are painting landscape on the spot, the arrangement of shapes and colours is dictated by nature, but with still life you are the one in control – you have a captive subject. You can set up the group in any way you choose, decide on the best lighting and take as long as you like over the

Setting up the group
(Above) *In still-life painting, much of the composition is done before you begin to lay paint on paper, so it is wise to take time at this stage. In James Horton's oil painting* Still Life with Narcissi *the objects, the tablecloth and the background drapery have been arranged with great care. By overlapping the mortar and the flower vase, a link is established between them, while the pattern on the tablecloth draws the eye into the composition.*

Repeating colours
(Left) *Elizabeth Moore's lovely* Objects on a Table *(oil) is also carefully arranged, although she has aimed at a more natural-looking effect. When painting a wide assortment of objects, some unifying factor is needed, and here she has created relationships of colour by taking the mauve-blues through the painting.*

Pattern and viewpoint

(Right) *The viewpoint you choose for your still life depends on your personal approach and interests. Seen from above, objects become flattened to some extent, creating a clearer pattern than at eye level. In* Still Life with Aubergines *(oil) Robert Maxwell Wood has exploited this element to the full, choosing and arranging the objects so that they echo the bold motifs of the fabric – notice the pansy, which appears both as living flower and as printed pattern.*

Composing with light

(Below right) *Light and shadow can play a vital role in any still life illuminated by natural light, and in* Lilies and Straw Hat *(oil) by Timothy Easton the shapes made by the shadow of the window bars and flowers are as important as the objects themselves. The use of carefully controlled, pale colours, with the only dark tone being the foliage glimpsed through the window, beautifully expresses the theme of light, which is further illustrated by the hat in the foreground – sunlight by association.*

CHOOSING A THEME

Most still lifes have some kind of theme, with the objects linked by association. An ill-assorted group of objects with nothing in common creates an uneasy feeling – the Surrealist painters used odd juxtapositions for this very reason. Still lifes with a culinary theme are a common choice: for example, fruit and vegetables placed on a kitchen table.

But the theme can be simply one of colour or shape. For example, you might choose a group of predominantly blue objects, placed on a yellow or pink cloth for contrast. You might be attracted by the vertical emphasis of bottles, or long-stemmed flowers in a tall vase, or be interested in an arrangement of plates and bowls which make a series of intersecting circles and ovals.

Still lifes can also tell a story, or hint at one. Artists may choose a subject close to their hearts, or something which has associations for them, such as favourite books, or a hat worn during a successful holiday. Van Gogh, when he was working as a peasant in the fields, painted a pair of battered, work-stained boots, which spoke volumes about the desperation of his life at the time.

painting. You are not at the mercy of the weather, as you are with landscape; indeed, still life is something you can always fall back on when it is too cold, wet or dark to paint anything else.

ARRANGING THE GROUP

It must be said that still life is not an easy option. You have to take as much care over choosing and arranging the objects as you do over painting them. Cézanne, who produced some of the most beautiful still lifes in the history of art, sometimes spent days over the initial arrangement.

Try to aim at a natural-looking grouping of the objects; although still life is highly artificial, it should not look that way. Let

Floral still life

(Left) *The foreground can be a problem in floral groups, as the spaces beside and in front of the vase can become dull and empty if they are not filled in some way. Common devices are to introduce some other object or place one or two of the blooms in front of the vase, and in Ben Baker's colourful* Still Life with Flowers *(oil) he has done both. He has treated the foreground very broadly, however, so that the objects are mere suggestions and do not detract from the painting's centre of interest, which is emphasized by the use of a dark background.*

some of the objects overlap, but be careful how you do this. Avoid obscuring one shape with another or leaving too small a part of one showing, as this can create an awkward, cramped feeling.

Consider too the spaces between things – wide gaps between objects may make them look disconnected, in which case some kind of link needs to be established. Depending on the source of light, shadows can provide a link between objects; another well-known device is drapery, often seen in still lifes, curving round behind, between and in front of objects to unite them.

Drapery also gives a sense of movement to the group. In any good painting, whatever the subject, the composition is arranged to lead the eye from one part of the picture to another. For this reason, avoid placing objects so that they "look" out of the picture. If the spout of a teapot,

for example, is pointing outwards instead of inwards towards the other objects, the eye will naturally follow its direction.

PLANNING THE PAINTING

It often happens that a group that has taken time to set up causes problems when you start to paint, or to make your preliminary drawing. You may now notice that one object is too tall, giving you a featureless area of background on both sides of it, or that there are too many objects crowded to the front. You can always make adjustments; it is better to get things right before you have gone too far than to paint something you don't like.

Once satisfied with the arrangement, you must consider how you are going to place it on the canvas. This means deciding what angle to paint from, what viewpoint to take and how much space to leave around the

Unusual treatments

(Above) *One of the exciting aspects of still-life painting is that the objects you choose can often suggest new approaches, in terms both of composition and treatment. Gerry Baptist initially chose this bunch of onions for his acrylic painting* Red Onions *because he liked their rich colours, but their shapes suggested movement, so he has arranged them in such a way that they appear to be rushing across the paper, an effect he has played up by using strong shadows and long, sweeping brushstrokes.*

Found still life

(Below) *Although most still-life paintings are the result of planning, occasionally something makes a natural painting subject. Examples could be clothes left on a chair, shoes in the corner of a room – indeed almost anything in your home environment. In his oil painting,* Decorated Tree, *Robert Maxwell Wood studies shapes, colours and textures not normally associated with still-life painting.*

objects. If your group is on a table top and the front of the table is in the picture, it is best to avoid a straight-on view, as this creates a horizontal in the foreground. Horizontal lines give a static impression, whereas diagonals lead the eye inwards, so study the group from different angles.

It can be interesting to look down slightly on the group you are painting, particularly when circles (plates and bowls) are an important part of the theme. From a high viewpoint, you see a rounder ellipse – the term for a circle in perspective – than you do at eye level. The viewpoint you choose depends very much on what you are painting; experiment with high and low viewpoints as well as different angles. Some artists find it helpful to settle all these questions before they begin to paint by making a series of rough sketches of the group, seen in various ways.

Outdoor still life

(Above) *A still life can be broadly defined as anything that is not capable of movement, so it follows that you may find ready-made groups outside as well as in your home. Stones on a beach, plant pots, a group of chairs in a garden, or glasses and bottles on a café table are just some of the many possibilities. In* East End Pipes *(oil) Karen Raney has found an exciting and unusual subject which has allowed her to explore strong contrasts of tone and relationships between shapes and colours.*

STILL-LIFE DEMONSTRATION

O
I
L

&

A
C
R
Y
L
I
C

James Horton regards himself primarily as a landscape painter, although he also paints portraits and often turns to still life when the weather does not permit outdoor landscape work. He enjoys still-life painting because it allows him total control of the subject, enabling him to work out ideas on composition and colour. He works in oil on a small scale, painting on canvases he prepares himself by stretching cotton fabric over board. They are then primed with a home-made recipe consisting mainly of whiting and rabbit-skin size.

1 (Right) *The artist dislikes working on white canvas, so, after priming, he tints it with a wash of watercolour. He has chosen a warm yellow ground colour which will help to establish the overall colour scheme. For the initial drawing, made with a fine sable brush, he uses an equally warm red-brown.*

3 *Light and dark tones must be related in the same way, and the highlight of the grapefruit provides a key for judging the strength of colours needed for the apple.*

2 (Above) *He begins by placing brush-strokes over the entire picture surface, working up the foreground and background at the same time in order to relate one colour to another.*

4 *Here, a painting knife is used, not to apply paint but to scrape it off, thus blending and softening the colours on the edge of the plate.*

5 *The pattern of the plate is drawn in with a fine sable brush. This stage also demonstrates the positive role played by the coloured ground, patches of which show through the light, cool, neutral colours.*

6 With the pattern complete, highlights have been added to the plate, but the ground is still visible in places and will not be completely covered, even in the final stages.

7 Too much detail in the background would detract from that in the foreground, so the artist suggests the pattern with small dabs of the brush. The pattern of holes in the weave of the basket was created by working small brushstrokes of light green over the brown.

8 For the final details on the basket, the painting is turned upside-down to give better access to this area, and a fine sable brush is used to touch in the lines of the weave.

9 (Below) In the finished painting, small patches of the coloured ground are still clearly visible, particularly in the blue-green foreground. This has the effect of linking this area with the warm colours of the background and objects.

LANDSCAPE

Landscapes need not be painted on the spot – many fine paintings are made from sketches and photographic reference – but when weather permits there is nothing more enjoyable than working direct from the subject out of doors.

Both oil and acrylic are excellent for outdoor work. With acrylic, of course, the paints could dry out on your palette before you are halfway through but, if you use a Stay-Wet palette, this will not happen. The advantage is that the painting will be completely dry when you want to stop work; you can also work on paper instead of canvas or board if you prefer. With oil,

Leading the eye

(Above) *A good landscape gives you the feeling that you can walk into and around it, so the artist must consider ways of leading the eye into the picture. A common device is to use a curving path or river travelling from foreground to middle distance, and in* Vineyard in the Languedoc (oil) *Madge Bright has used the lines of the vineyard in the same way, so that they act as signposts towards the painting's centre of interest: the group of houses.*

Restricting the space

(Left) *The word landscape generally conjures up an image of a wide panorama or perhaps a dramatic mountain view, but anything that is out of doors is a landscape; for those who have no access to open countryside, parks and gardens are an excellent choice. Restricting himself to a landscape in microcosm in his* View of Back Gardens, *Ben Baker has achieved a lively composition in which he has explored contrasts of colour, shape and texture.*

Human interest

(Opposite) *Another way of drawing the eye into the painting is to introduce a figure or figures in the middle distance, as David Curtis has done in* Poppyfield over Misson (oil). *It is a curious fact that, because of the way we identify with them, fellow humans always attract attention. The other function of figures in landscape is to provide scale; here they emphasize the wide expanse of poppy-strewn field.*

Creating space
(Right) *If you are
painting a small section
of landscape in close-up
you do not have to
worry unduly about
creating a sense of space,
but in a panoramic
landscape like Timothy
Easton's* The Ploughed
Edge *it is vital. He has
done this in two main
ways: firstly by
exploiting the
perspective effect of the
converging lines of
ploughing; and secondly
by using paler, slightly
cooler colours in the
distance.*

you will always have a wet painting to carry home, which can be a problem if the painting is large and it is a windy day.

PLANNING THE PICTURE
One of the commonest faults in paintings done on the spot is poor composition –

sometimes even professionals get it wrong. First you must decide what format your painting should take and, secondly, how much of the view you should include.

A further advantage of working with acrylic on paper is that you can let the composition grow "organically". Without much time for planning, because of changing light and so on, mistakes can easily occur; when you are well into a painting you often find that you should have included a certain tree on the right, for example, or made the picture vertical instead of horizontal. The answer is to take a larger piece of paper than you need and leave generous margins when you begin to work; this allows you greater flexibility and the freedom to make any necessary changes.

You cannot do this with oil paintings, unfortunately, because they have to be fitted into the confines of your canvas or board. It is wise to take several working surfaces with you so that you can decide which one best suits the subject. Using a

The foreground

(Right) *This can be a problem area in landscape paintings. Because this part of the view is closest to you it is seen in sharp focus, so the natural tendency is to treat it in detail. This can, however, be unwise, as it can act as a block, discouraging the viewer from looking beyond it into the picture. In Timothy Easton's* Dwarf Firs and Cottage *(oil) he has solved the problem by contriving a strong focal point – the figure in front of the house – so that although the foreground flowers claim attention first, the eye then travels over and beyond them.*

Cropping the foreground

(Above) *Sometimes the foreground in a landscape serves to introduce the view beyond, with a focal point in the middle distance, but it can be the raison d'être of the painting, as in Gerry Baptist's* On the Coast of Provence *(acrylic). In order to create space and recession he has employed a traditional compositional device, that of cropping the trees at the top and bottom of the picture. This has the effect of bringing them to the front of the picture, while everything beyond recedes.*

viewfinder is also a good idea, to help you to decide how much of the scene to include. This device is easily made by cutting a rectangular aperture in a piece of card; you can then hold it up at different angles and at different distances from your eyes in order to isolate various sections of the landscape. This can help when you are faced with a wide panoramic view and you cannot decide which bit to focus on, or where the centre of interest lies.

THE FOCAL POINT

Most landscapes have a centre of interest, or focal point, to which the eye is drawn. How obvious this is depends on the scene. Examples of an obvious focal point might include a group of buildings in a landscape, a tall tree, or some people sitting down having a picnic – people always grab our attention because we identify with our

fellow humans. A less obvious focal point might be a ploughed field making a pattern in the middle distance, a particular hill, a gleam of light on a lake or river, or a light tree set against darker ones.

Try to orchestrate the painting so that you set up a series of visual signposts towards the focal point. These will probably already exist, although you may have to exaggerate them. Diagonal lines or curves invite the eye to follow them, and a device frequently used in landscape is a curving path leading from the foreground in towards the middle distance – where the focal point is often located. Alternatives are receding lines of trees, lines of ploughed fields or the stripes of a newly cut hay field. Do not make the foreground too dominant. If the focal point is in the middle distance or the far distance, too much detail in the foreground will detract from it.

CREATING SPACE

A landscape will not look convincing unless you give the impression of space, and there are two principal ways of doing this. One is to observe the effects of linear perspective correctly. Everyone knows that things become smaller the further away they are, but it is easy to underestimate this effect. You know that a field or a far-away lake is a certain size and you fail to realize that it is actually tiny in relation to the rest of your picture. It is wise to measure such landscape features when you make your preliminary drawing. Hold a pencil or paintbrush up at arm's length and slide your finger and thumb up and down it; in this way you can establish the size of the distant lake in comparison, for example, with a field which is closer.

The other way to create space is to use aerial perspective. Tiny particles of dust in the atmosphere create an effect rather like a series of ever-thickening veils, so that far-away objects are paler than nearby ones. There is far less contrast of tone (light and dark) and the colours change, becoming cooler and bluer. Again, this effect is easy to underestimate, particularly for features in the middle distance. You know that a tree trunk on the other side of a field is dark brown, so you paint it that way but, in fact, it will be much lighter in tone than it would be if it were in the foreground.

When it comes to far distance, colours can be very pale, although sometimes they appear dark in relation to a still-lighter sky. The contrasts of tone are minimal, sometimes barely distinguishable. A ray of sunshine lighting up part of a distant hill looks dramatic, but the tonal contrast is still relatively limited. These subtle nuances of colour and tone can be tricky, but with practice you will master them.

Controlling tones

(Left) *Patrick Cullen's* Landscape in Provence *is first and foremost a painting of light, with the landscape illuminated by the soft, pearly glow of early morning. This reduces contrasts of tone, so the relative lightness and darkness of colours must be controlled extremely carefully. Notice that there are no dark colours here – even the foreground tree and railings are pale whispers of golden brown and green, and the composition is unified by the repetition of delicate mauves, yellows and golds.*

Light and colour

(Below) *The effects of light can completely transform a landscape: colours that looked vivid on a sunny day may seem flat and dull under an overcast sky, and the differences between evening light and a high midday sun are equally striking. Stewart Geddes's lovely* Le Rocher Dongle, Evening *(oil) is as much about light as it is about the landscape itself, and the artist has wisely treated both the buildings and the landscape features very broadly to give full rein to the golden evening colours.*

LANDSCAPE DEMONSTRATION

Karen Raney is an experimental artist who works in a number of media and paints a variety of different subjects – indeed, anything which excites her interest. Although she works direct from the subject whenever possible, she also uses photographs as an extensive reference; here she re-creates a landscape from her own photographs, aided by memories of the place, which she has painted many times. She is working in oil on a commercially prepared stretched and primed canvas.

1 *Brushwork is an important element in this landscape, and the artist has begun to exploit it immediately, employing a flat bristle brush to make sweeping strokes of paint diluted with turpentine.*

2 *Once the composition has been established with the diluted paint, she begins to use it more thickly, adding a little linseed oil to the turpentine and painting darker colours into the thin washes.*

3 *Colours are smeared and blended together with a fingertip. She likes to move paint around as she works, and oil paint, which remains wet for a considerable time, encourages such manipulation.*

4 (Right) *To create the rounded blobs of the trees, a bristle brush is loaded with paint, pushed onto the picture surface and twisted slightly. The paint is then built up more solidly all over the picture; here it is used straight from the tube, with no added medium. Notice the way in which the artist uses the brush-marks to describe the shapes of the roof tiles.*

6 (Above) *She takes a less deliberate approach to painting than some artists, letting the picture dictate what she should do next, and experimenting to see what happens. Here she uses upward-sweeping brushstrokes once more, later modifying them slightly.*

5 (Above) *The artist has wiped into the thin paint with a rag to create a striated effect, which she now reinforces with thick white brushstrokes. She works instinctively, seeing that the sweeping roof lines need to be echoed in this area of the painting.*

7 (Right) *Having built up the middle ground and distance, she returns to the foreground and introduces darker, richer colours into the roof, using the side of a flat bristle brush to suggest the shadowed divisions between the tiles.*

Continued ▷

8 The distant village, which is the focal point of the picture, is left until a late stage; it is now treated in the same way as the rest of the painting, with bold brushstrokes describing the shapes and forms.

9 The brushwork depicting the houses can be seen clearly here – vertical strokes for the walls and horizontal for the roofs. The hills behind are now built up more decisively.

10 A fingernail scratches into the light paint to reveal a little of the darker colour beneath, which is now completely dry.

11 It is important to create visual links between one part of the picture and another, and a little of the light green in the middle ground is now taken into the blue of the hills.

12 (Right) *Strokes of thick, light paint are swept across the sky, with sufficient pressure applied to the broad flat brush to create a series of tiny ridges in each stroke.*

13 (Above) *The finished painting illustrates beautifully what is meant by creating a sense of movement in a composition. The eye is led into and around the painting by the wing-like shape of the foreground roof and by the directional brushwork.*

FIGURES & PORTRAITS

The human figure, whether painted as a portrait, a full-length study, a clothed figure or a nude, presents a greater challenge to the artist than any other subject. A still life may be quite satisfactory even if the ellipse on a vase or plate is not right or the table top is out of perspective. But in figure painting such things do matter – we are all familiar with the general structure and proportions of our fellow humans.

It has to be said that the human figure is not easy to portray; the interaction of forms is complex and subtle. Figure and portrait work relies on drawing as much as on painting. This does not mean that you must make a painstaking and detailed drawing and then fill it in, but you must think about the underlying structure – the drawing – all the time as you work and be prepared to make corrections. Working in opaque paints is a considerable advantage here. With oil you can scrape areas back and repaint them, while with acrylic you can easily correct the drawing by overpainting.

STUDYING THE SUBJECT

Drawing the nude is one of the best ways of studying the figure, and even if you intend to paint only portraits and clothed figures it pays to join a life class. It is not essential, however. What is important is to practise drawing people whenever you can. Ask friends to pose for you; draw yourself in the mirror; take a sketchbook with you and make studies of people walking in the street, sitting at café tables, reading or simply relaxing.

PLANNING THE PICTURE

Whether you are painting a head-and-shoulders portrait, a full-length portrait or a nude figure study, never lose sight of the fact that you are also producing a picture.

Form and brushwork

(Above) *As the human face and head are complex and difficult to paint, even before you have considered how to achieve a likeness of the sitter, there is a tendency to draw lines with a small brush. This is seldom satisfactory, however, as hard lines can destroy the form. In Ted Gould's* Sue *(oil), the features, although perfectly convincing, are described with the minimum of detail and no use of line, and the forms of face, hair and clothing are built up with broad directional brushwork.*

Form and colour

(Right) *As a general rule, the colours in shadows are cooler, that is, bluer or greener, than those in the highlight areas, and Gerry Baptist has skilfully exploited this warm/cool contrast to give solidity to the head in his acrylic* Self Portrait. *Although all the colours are heightened, they are nevertheless based on the actual colours of flesh, and the picture is successful in its own terms.*

Painting in monochrome

(Left) *In this unusual oil painting,* Self Portrait at 32 Years, *Gerald Cains has taken a diametrically opposite approach to Gerry Baptist and ruled out colour altogether, while using highly expressive brushwork. The effect is extraordinarily powerful. It can be a useful discipline to work in monochrome, as it helps you to concentrate on composition and tonal balance without the distraction of colour.*

In a portrait, particularly, the desire to achieve a likeness can be so all-consuming that you may forget about all the other aspects of the painting.

Much the same applies to figure paintings. The model is often placed right in the middle of the canvas or, worse still, with the feet cropped off at the ankles because they would not fit in. Too much attention is given to the figure and not enough to any other elements in the picture, such as the background. This is understandable, as the figure is the most difficult thing to paint, but it gives a disjointed effect – a good composition is one in which everything is given equal consideration.

Colour and mood

(Left) *Portraiture involves more than simply achieving a likeness through correct observation of the shapes of noses, eyes and mouths. The best portraits give a feeling of atmosphere and express something of the sitter's character. In Karen Raney's* David *a sense of melancholy and introspection is conveyed through the sombre colours and heavy, downward-sweeping brushmarks as well as by the sitter's intense but inward-looking gaze.*

Composing a figure study
(Left) *In a figure painting you must decide where to place the figure, whether or not to crop part of it, and whether you need to introduce other elements as a balance. Peter Clossick's* Helen Seated *gives the impression of spontaneity because it is so boldly and thickly painted, but it is carefully composed, with the diagonal thrust of the figure balanced by verticals and opposing diagonals in the background.*

Before you start to paint, consider how you are going to place the head or figure on the canvas. A central placing generally looks stiff and unnatural, as does a direct, face-on approach. Heads in portraits are usually placed slightly off-centre, with the sitter viewed from a three-quarter angle; one shoulder thus appears higher than the other. In this case, more space is often left on the side towards which the sitter is looking, and the near shoulder is sometimes cropped by the canvas edge. Consider how much space to leave above the head. Too much and the head can appear pushed down; too little and it will seem cramped.

LIGHTING
Lighting is vital in portraiture and figure work. The play of light and shade not only describes the forms but also provides the all-important element of tonal contrast. If you look at a face under a harsh, direct light, it looks flat and dull with very little depth, but if the light comes from one side it strikes parts of the face while throwing others into shadow, immediately creating a more interesting configuration. The form of lighting most favoured for portrait and figure work is called three-quarter lighting – the illumination comes from one side,

slightly to the front of the model, thus lighting three-quarters of the face and body.

If you can control the lighting set-up, think also about the strength of the light. Those who paint out of doors will have noticed that bright sunlight casts very positive, heavy shadows. Although strong light can create dramatic effects in a portrait and many artists deliberately choose it, it is not suitable for all subjects. In a painting of a young woman or child, for example, a diffused light is more suitable, as this brings out the subtlety of the flesh tones. If you are painting by a window, you might consider some form of diffuser, such as a net curtain or tracing paper placed over the window. Over-hard shadows on one side of the face can also be lightened by using a reflector. By propping up a white board or piece of paper by the side of your sitter, opposite the source of light, you can bounce some light back onto the dark side of the face, giving touches of colour to the shadow while still preserving tonal contrast.

Painting children
(Right) *Painting an adult engaged in some typical pursuit can enhance your interpretation, but in the case of children it is a question of necessity; they seldom remain still for long, added to which they look stiff and self-conscious when artificially posed. In her delightful, light-suffused study of* Samantha and Alexis *(oil) Karen Raney has worked rapidly to capture a moment of communication between her two young subjects.*

THE FIGURE IN CONTEXT

In a head-and-shoulders portrait, the background is frequently left deliberately vague and undefined in order to focus attention on the face, but a whole figure must be put into a believable context, so some of the room should be included. If you are painting the nude in a life class, you may not have much control over background and other elements, but for a clothed figure painted in your own home or theirs, you will have a wider choice. Particular props are often used in portraiture to help describe the character and interests of the sitter. A writer or someone fond of reading might be shown with a selection of favourite books, or a musician with his or her instrument. Try to convey something of the atmosphere surrounding your sitter.

Full-length portraits

(Above) *When you intend to paint the whole figure rather than just a head and shoulders, you must consider what other elements to include and what props will help to enhance your description of the sitter. If you are painting the subject in their own home, you can show them in familiar surroundings and with personal possessions, as David Curtis has done in his lovely* Interior with Jacqueline (oil), *which is both a portrait and a visual essay on light.*

Outdoor settings

(Right) *Light is also an important element in Timothy Easton's* The Summer Read *and, like David Curtis, he has described the sitter more by posture, clothing and general shape than by detailed depiction of features, indeed the features are barely visible. With careful observation, you will find that it is perfectly possible to paint a recognizable likeness of a person without showing the face at all.*

INDEX

Stockists & Suppliers

Australia and New Zealand

ACT Paper Pty Ltd
10 McGlore Street
Micham
Victoria 3132

E & F Good
31 Landsdowne Terrace
Walkerville SA 5081

Kaori Art and Craft Centre
264 Karon Road
Kaori
New Zealand

United Kingdom

Binney & Smith
(Liquitex UK)
Ampthill Road
Bedford MK 42 9RS

Cornelissen & Son Ltd
105 Great Russel Street
London WC1B 3RY

Daler-Rowney Ltd
PO Box 10
Southern Industrial Estate
Bracknell
Berkshire RG12 8ST

John Mathieson & Co.
48 Frederick Street
Edinburgh H2 1HG

Russel & Chapple Ltd
Canvas & Art Materials
23 Monmouth Street
London WC2H 9DE

Winsor & Newton
Whitefriars Avenue
Wealdstone, Harrow
Middlesex HA3 5RH

United States

Art Supply Warehouse
360 Main Avenue
Norwalk, CT 06851
(mail order)

Binney & Smith Artist's
Materials
1100 Church Lane
PO Box 431
Easton, PA 18042

Boncour Artist's Colors Inc.
Zipatone Inc.
150 Fence Lane
Hillside IL 60162

Chromacryl (Australia)
US Distributor
Chrome Acrylics
40 Tanner Street
Haddonfield, NJ 08033

Daniel Smith Inc.
Fine Arts Materials
4130 First Avenue South
Seattle, WA 98134

NY Central Art Supply
62 Third Avenue
New York, NY 10003

Pearl Paint Corporation
308 Canal Street
New York, NY 10013

Standard Brands Paint
Company
4300 West 190th Street
Torrance CA 90509-2956

Utrecht Manufacturing
Corporation
33 35th Street
Brooklyn, NY 11232

Winsor & Newton, Inc.
US Office
11 Commission Avenue
PO Box 1396
Piscataway, NJ 08033

NOTES

NOTES

NOTES

NOTES